Simply Delicious Wheat & Gluten Free *Cooking*

A light and fun compilation of recipes which have been perfected over the last nine years in my wheat and gluten free kitchen.

CENTRAL COAST PRESS

San Luis Obispo, California

ISBN 1-930401-28-0

CENTRAL COAST PRESS
P.O. Box 3654
San Luis Obispo, California

Dedication

To my late husband

Paul Seager

He would be so proud that

I finally finished the book.

Acknowledgments

My precious grand daughter, Amelia Christine Cole, who submitted her 4-H award winning recipe for Deviled Eggs.

Jeanette Cole, giggle-mate and beyond. Cover photo by Jeanette.

Dane Mark Svenningsen, cover design.

Tracy Vidal, soon to be Tracy Vidal-Miller, the photo guru.

All of those "gluten eaters" who tested the goodies lying herein.

David F. Frankel, M.D.

Mostly, to my sons and their wives...if this was the story of Noah, in the book of Genesis, I would name my sons but not their wives, but this is not the Holy Bible... the girls in my life are Holly, Jeanette and Michelle.

Introduction

At the time of my diagnosis in 1995, I was pathetically sick... a story, like many others, of a long history of misdiagnosis.

Fortunately for me, meetings of the San Diego chapter of CSA were held in a library just minutes from my home. The people were warm and welcoming. It was there at those meetings that I obtained the greatest amount of clear information on Celiac Disease and the gluten free diet.

It was at this time too, that wonderful bean flour was produced. It was sold in a small health food store nearby. Since I knew very little about alternative flours but a lot about cooking, my thought was, "I'll give it a whirl." Today the bean flour is still whirling in my kitchen. You will find it called for in many of the recipes.

Through these past years, my recipes have been "taste tested" by people who can eat anything. It was very important to know that the food still tasted good! It is my hope that you will spend time in the kitchen and enjoy your new diet. Gluten free cooking need not be a mystery anymore.

Every photo in this book is of real food, made in my kitchen...eaten by anyone who was hungry...even after we had taken 28 pictures and the food was cold! It was still simply delicious.

I decided not to have a doctor endorse my book, since it took over 14 years for one of them to diagnose me properly. However, I do bow to Dr. David F. Frankel, of Sansum Medical Clinic in Santa Barbara, California for saving my life.

Enjoy cooking, enjoy eating.

To your good health!

Banquet Table of Contents

Dedication 3
Acknowledgements 4
Introduction 5
Just the Basics 9
Prepare Yourself 10
Gluten Free Kitchen Basics 12
The Basic Three Mixes 13
Shopper's Guide 14
Sauces 17
Florentine Sauce 18
Lasagna Sauce 19
Alfredo Sauce 20
Marinara Sauce 21
Measuring 22
Quick Breads 23
Apple Muffin 24
Blueberry Muffin Tops 25
Lemon Yogurt Poppy Seed 26
Miner's Pan Cake 27
Waffles 28
Pancakes 29
10 Minute Cake Doughnuts 30
Apple Cobbler Crisp 31
Banana Bread 32
Corn Bread or Corn Bread Muffins 33
Biscuits 34
Mustard Biscuits with Sesame Seeds 35
About Bread Crumbs 36
Yeast Breads 37
Crowning White Bread 38
Dark *Rye Bread 39
Golden Almond Bread Machine Method 40
Light *Rye Bread Machine Method 41
Hamburger Buns/Sandwich Rolls/Baguettes 42
French Bread 43
Pizza Dough 44
Eggs & Other Breakfast Choices 45
Amelia's Deviled Eggs 46
Buckwheat Cereal 47
French Toast 48
Eggs Ole 49
Huevos Rancheros 50
Bread Pudding 51
Chile Relleno Casserole 52
Cranberry Orange Sticky Buns 53
Ham and Cheese Casserole 54
Seafood Omelet 55
Aebelskiver (Danish Pancakes) 56
Salads & Dressings 59
Spinach Salad 60

Coleslaw.... 61
South of the Border Salad.... 62
Grilled Chicken Caesar Salad.... 63
Pasta Spirals with Raspberry Dressing and Fruit.... 64
Cantaloupe & Curried Chicken Salad.... 65
Chinese Chicken Salad/ Dressing.... 66
Croutons.... 67
Vegetable Pasta Salad.... 68
Soups.... 69
Cream of Celery Soup.... 70
Cream of Chicken Soup.... 71
Cream of Mushroom Soup.... 72
Pasta y Frigoli – Italian Lentil Soup with Pasta.... 73
French Onion Soup.... 74
12 Minute Cream of Tomato Soup.... 75
Sandwiches.... 77
Ham and Cheese Sub.... 78
Tuna Salad for Sandwiches.... 79
Egg Salad.... 80
Salmon Salad.... 81
Pastrami on *Rye.... 82
Peanut Butter and Jelly.... 83
Cooking Instructions for Asian Noodles.... 84
Pastas.... 85
Introduction to Pastas.... 86
3 Cheese Macaroni Bake.... 89
Pasta Pizza Salad.... 90
Spinach Stuffed Lasagna Rolls.... 91
Lasagna with Meat Sauce.... 92
Spaghetti and Meatballs.... 93
Lemon Linguini.... 94
Spaghetti All'uova or Poor Man's Spaghetti.... 95
Crab and Shrimp Sea Shell Pasta Salad.... 96
COLOR PHOTOS.... 97-112
Potato & Rice Dishes.... 113
Risotto.... 114
Twice Baked Potatoes with Zip.... 115
San Diego Mashed Potatoes.... 116
Creamy Potatoes and Broccoli Bake.... 117
Two-timing Rice and Potatoes.... 118
Garlic Mashed Potatoes.... 119
Dilled Potato Salad.... 120
Potato Wedges.... 121
Scalloped Potatoes.... 122
Sour Cream and Onion Bake.... 123
Main Dishes.... 125
Swiss Steak Bake.... 126
Stuffed Peppers.... 127
Deviled Pork Chops.... 128
Baked Salmon in Dill Sauce.... 129
Italian Sausage Stuffed Mushrooms.... 130
Basic Meatloaf.... 131
Meat and Bean Burritos.... 132
Chicken Florentine.... 133

San Luis Obispo Chicken Chile Relleno........ 134
Green Chile Chicken........ 135
Pork Roast and Gravy........ 136
Fish and Chips........ 137
Eggplant Parmesan........ 138
Beef Stroganoff........ 139
Shrimp and Fish Au Gratin........ 140

Slow Cook........ 141
Turkey Mexicana........ 142
Pot Roast........ 143
High Sierra Pot Roast........ 144
Chinese Chicken........ 145
Pork Chile Verde........ 146
Slow Cook-Corned Beef Dinner........ 147

Cakes, Cookies & other Sweets........ 149
Morro Rock Bundt Cake........ 150
Applesauce Bundt Cake........ 151
Carrot Cake........ 152
Mock Graham Cracker Crust........ 153
Flan (Carmel Custard)........ 154
Hazelnut Cookies (Filbertines)........ 155
3 Ingredient Almond Cookie........ 156
Piano Keys........ 157
Flour-Free Peanut Butter Chocolate Chip Cookies........ 158
Brownies........ 159
Raspberry Bars........ 160
Coconut Macaroons........ 161
Diamond Lil's Pecan Bar........ 162
Criss Cross Peanut Butter Cookies........ 164

Sweet Things........ 165
Crêpes........ 166
Crêpes Fillings........ 167
Crepes Syrup........ 168
English Toffee........ 169
Strawberry Ice........ 170

Beverages........ 171
Strawberry Banana Smoothie........ 172
Peaches & Cream Smoothie........ 172
Mocha Java Smoothie........ 173
Mock Kahlua........ 173
Mimosas........ 174
Iced Tea........ 174

Dips, Spreads & Snacks........ 175
San Francisco French Garlic Spread........ 176
Gilroy Garlic Growers Reply........ 176
Cheese Crackers with Flax Seeds........ 177
Buckwheat Thins........ 178
Party Wings........ 179
Crab Dip........ 180
Cottage Cheese and Dill Dip........ 180
Dill Pickles........ 181

Have Questions about Products?........ 182

Glossary of Terms........ 184

Index........ 189

Just the Basics

Prepare Yourself

Gluten Free Kitchen Basics

The Basic Three Mixes

Shopper's Guide

Prepare Yourself

A treasury of little hints for getting and staying healthy.

Now that you know there is a healing process and it is controlled by your diet, your life will become much easier. I know if you are newly diagnosed, this may seem far from being true, but it is.

The first thing that we have to face (while food shopping) is that we can't just throw familiar foods into the shopping cart. We must read the labels. Fortunately, labels are becoming more informative, giving us more detail in the processed foodstuff that we want to buy. Some national brand foods are even letting us know that their product is "gluten free".

Personally, I have a little credo; "When in doubt, I go without". So if the label does not tell me enough about the ingredients, it stays in the store.

Start your new diet simply. Find some good old comfort food recipes and see what you can do to make them GF. And yes, there is chocolate!

I am not a proponent of spending an entire day or an entire paycheck in a health-food store buying prepared GF foods that taste like cardboard. However, I am a stickler on the importance of maintaining a good tasting GF diet AND health food stores, Oriental markets, mail order and on-line shopping will offer up a wide variety of foods to make your conversions easier.

There is a Shopper's Guide on page 14.

Be creative and don't get discouraged if you make a mistake. I made a ton of mistakes. Follow this book's simple instructions...you can't go wrong.

When you make something wonderful, make more!

Be patient in your kitchen. It is far easier than being a patient out of your kitchen.

Baking is a little tricky at first. If you know another person who bakes GF, try to bake together.

Kitchen Tools for successful baking

- Non stick muffin pans; Muffin tops, mini muffins and full muffins
- Non stick cookie sheets
- Bread pans: Varying sizes and shapes, glass and non stick
- Cake pans: Squares and rounds, glass and non stick
- Pizza pans: Non-stick pans do well for a period of time, parchment paper on older pans works fine.
- Bread machine
- Waffle maker
- Electric mixer, free-standing or hand-held
- Double boiler, or equivalent
- Food chopper, graters
- Cups for dry and liquid measure
- Measuring spoons, spatulas, serving utensils for non-scratch surfaces, wire whisks and toothpicks for testing doneness.
- Mixing bowls: varying sizes
- Oven and microwave
- Doughnut pans
- **One good cookbook (this one!)**

Gluten Free Kitchen Basics

Make a place just for your gluten free baking products. A separate pantry shelf and see-through, airtight containers work very well. Everyone has a different method for planning his or her storage space, but for convenience sake, I offer that example.

After years of blending GF flours, the ones in this book are perfected to perform the best for all of my cooking needs. As the book title suggests, this is going to be simple. These are the only mixes that you will use throughout this book.

If you have space in your GF storage, it is handy to triple the bun and pizza mixes. They do not need to be refrigerated if sealed in an airtight container. *Then when you want pizza you will use 3 cups of mix to make 2-15" pizzas and 2¼ cups bun mix per batch of buns.*

Complete instructions on ways to use these mixes are found throughout the book.

GF

GF, when used in this book, means Gluten Free

Gluten Free always means Wheat Free

Wheat Free

The Basic Three Mixes

1	2	3
Bread Flour	Sandwich Rolls Hamburger Buns Baguettes	Pizza Dough

1. ***Bread Flour Mix*** (Yields 9 cups)

3 c. bean flour, Garfava ™
3 c. white rice flour
2 c. potato starch
1 c. tapioca starch
Xanthan gum must be added
Amounts will be noted in each recipe

2. ***Sandwich Roll and Hamburger Bun Mix*** (Yields 8 buns)

1 ½ c. white rice flour
½ c. potato starch
¼ c. tapioca starch
2 tsp. xanthan gum

3. ***Pizza Dough Mix***
(Yields 2-15 inch pizzas)

1 ½ c. white rice flour
1 c. tapioca starch
½ c. bean flour
1 Tbsp. xanthan gum

Her new recipe:
1c bean flr
1c w. rice
1c tapioca
1 tsp salt
2 Tbsp sugar
1½ c warm water - 1 pkg yeast
3 egg white
1 tsp vinegar
1½ T oil

All of these flours and xanthan gum can be bought on-line Shopper's Guide to follow.

Shopper's Guide

(Where to Find Wheat and Gluten-Free Baking Products)

Authentic Foods
(Garfava flour ™, brown and white rice flour, tapioca starch, almond meal, and potato starch, xanthan gum, maple sugar, vanilla powder, rye flavor powder) 1850 West 169th Street, Suite B, Gardena, CA 90247 Phone (800) 806-4737or (310) 366-7612 Order online: authenticfoods.com. I buy most of my baking goods here, however, it is important to know there are many other manufacturers who sell products that you will need in order to use other GF recipes.

Bob's Red Mill
5209 S.E. International Way, Milwaukie, OR 97222; phone (503) 654-3215 some products can be found in health food stores and in health sections of grocery stores.

Cybros Inc.
P.O. Box 851 Waukesha, WI53187-0851; phone (800) 876-2253. Products can be found in health food stores.

DE-RO-MA
(Food Intolerance Centre) *(Gluten-free flours)* 1118 Berlier, Laval, Quebec H7L 3R9, Canada; phone (514) 990-5694 or (800) 363-DIET.

Dietary Specialties Inc.
865 Centennial Ave., Piscataway, NJ 08854; phone (888) 636-8123.

El Peto Products
(Bean, rice, quinoa, millet, and other gluten-free flours) 41 Shoemaker Street, Kitchener, Ontario N2E 3G9, Canada; phone (800) 387-4064.

Enger-G Foods, Inc
(Xanthan gum, almond meal, and tapioca, bean, rice, and other gluten-free flours, plus, this company produces a good line of rice pastas). P.O. Box 24723, Seattle, WA 98124-0723; phone (800) 331-5222. Products can be found in some health food stores and specialty markets.

Flavorganics:
268 Doremus Ave, Newark, NJ 07105; phone (973)-344-8014. Flavorganics.com.

The Gluten Free Pantry, Inc.
P.O. Box 840, Glastonbury, CT 06033; phone (800) 291-8386.

Grain Process Enterprises, LTD
39 Golden Gate Court, Scarborough, Ontario M1P 3A4, Canada; phone (416) 291-3226

Jowar Foods
113 Hickory Street, Hereford, TX 79045; phone (806) 363-9070.

King Arthur Flour
P.O. Box 876, Norwich, VT 05055; phone (800) 827-6836.

Kinnikinnick Foods
10306-112 Street, Edmonton, Alberta T5K 1N1, Canada; phone (403) 424-2900, toll free 1-877-503-4466
Web site www.kinnikinnick.com.

Miss Roben's
P.O. Box 1149, Frederick, MD 21702; phone (800) 891-0083.

Nancy's Natural Food
(Gluten-free flours including sorghum and bean, xanthan and guar gums, milk powders and substitutes):
266 N.W. First Avenue, Ste A, Canby, OR 97013; phone (503) 266-330.

The Really Great Food Co.
(Rice and tapioca flours, xanthan gum) P.O. Box 319, Malverne, NY 11565; phone (800) 593-5377.

Son's Milling
Unit #23, 6809 Kirkpatrick Crescent, Fanichiton, BC V8M 1Z8, Canada; phone (250) 544-1733.

Specialty Food Shop
Radio Centre Plaza, Upper Level, 875 Main Street West, Hamilton, Ontario L8S 4P9, Canada; phone (800) SFS-7976 or (905) 528-4707.

Up-to-date at the time of writing... a place to start.

Your Favorites

Supplier Name:

Phone:

Product:

Website:

Supplier Name:

Phone:

Product:

Website:

Supplier Name:

Phone:

Product:

Website:

Supplier Name:

Phone:

Product:

Website:

Supplier Name:

Phone:

Product:

Website:

Supplier Name:

Phone:

Product:

Website:

Supplier Name:

Phone:

Product:

Website:

Supplier Name:

Phone:

Product:

Website:

Supplier Name:

Phone:

Product:

Website:

Sauces

Florentine Sauce

Lasagna Sauce

Alfredo Sauce

Marinara Sauce

❖ Florentine Sauce ❖

3 Tbsp. butter
½ c. chopped green onions
½ c. finely chopped ham
1 ½ c. milk
10 oz frozen chopped spinach
(thawed and drained)
or 10 oz fresh chopped spinach
2 Tbsp.potato starch
½ c. water

Heat butter in a pot, add green onions and ham, stir in milk and heat until bubbly.

Mix together potato starch and water, add to pot and stir until thickened. Turn off heat and add spinach. Stir until all spinach is coated.

Can be made ahead and chilled for later use.

❖ *Lasagna Sauce* ❖

1 lb. ground round
1 lb. mild Italian sausage
1 lg. can crushed tomatoes
2 (8 oz.) cans tomato sauce
3 cloves crushed garlic
1 large bay leaf
1 Tbsp.dry Italian seasonings
1 c. water
Salt and pepper to taste

Brown meats and drain off excess liquids. Return to pan. Add tomatoes, sauce and seasonings. Simmer for ½ hour or more.

This recipe will make 1 large lasagna.

Serves 8-10

❖ Alfredo Sauce ❖

3 Tbsp.butter
8 fluid ounces heavy whipping cream
½ c. grated parmesan cheese
or parmesan/romano blend
1 egg yolk
2 Tbsp.grated parmesan cheese
Salt to taste

Melt butter or margarine in a saucepan over medium heat. Add heavy cream, stirring constantly. Stir in salt, grated parmesan cheese. Stir constantly until melted, then mix in egg yolk. Simmer over medium low heat for 3-5 minutes. Garnish with additional grated parmesan cheese, if desired.

Makes 2 servings

❖ Marinara Sauce ❖

1 lg. can crushed tomatoes
1 tsp. Italian seasoning (dried)
1 bay leaf
2 cloves garlic, crushed
1 Tbsp. olive oil

Heat olive oil in medium size saucepan, add garlic, bay leaf and seasoning, stir for about a minute to release the flavors.

Stir in tomatoes and simmer for at least 20 minutes.

This is a very light sauce and is good alone on your favorite rice pasta.

Makes 3 c.

Measuring

Measure all ingredients carefully. You will need two types of measuring cups; liquid and dry, it is difficult to measure dry ingredients accurately with liquid measures. **It is easier to measure peanut butter and shortenings in dry measuring cups.**

Liquid measuring cups are either glass or clear plastic, graduated sizes

Dry measuring cups are sold in sets of 5 nested cups, one eighth, one fourth, one third, one half and one cup.

Measuring spoons are usually sold in sets of 5, one eighth, one fourth, one third, one half and one teaspoon, and 1 tablespoon. **Pinch, Dash and Smidgen are sold in sets of 3**

Measuring Equivalents		
1 cup	16 Tbsp.	8 oz.
½ cup	8 Tbsp.	4 oz.
1/3 cup	5 Tbsp.+1 tsp.	2.7 oz
¼ cup	4 Tbsp.	2 oz.
1/8 cup	2 Tbsp.	1 oz.
1 Tbsp.	3 tsp.	½ oz.

Quick Breads

Apple Muffins

Blueberry Muffin Tops

Lemon Yogurt Poppy Seed Muffins

Miners Pan Cake

Waffles

Pancakes

10 Minute Cake Doughnuts

Apple Cobbler Crisp

Banana Bread

Corn Bread or Corn Bread Muffins

Biscuits

Mustard Biscuits with Sesame Seeds

Bread Crumbs

❖ Apple Muffins ❖

1 c. GF bread flour mix (p. 13)
¼ tsp. Xanthan gum
1 tsp. baking powder
¼ tsp. vanilla powder or 1 tsp. GF vanilla
3 Tbsp.sugar
¼ tsp. salt
½ c. applesauce
¼ tsp. cinnamon
1 lg. egg
1 Tbsp.vegetable oil
1 tsp. milk (or apple juice)

Combine all dry ingredients in a medium size bowl. Mix egg, oil, milk or juice, and applesauce. Add to dry ingredients.

Stir together, but do not over stir.

Divide mixture into 6 lightly buttered, or paper lined muffin cups.

Bake 350°, 12 minutes for (muffin top pans) or 15 minutes for (cup cake size).

Check for doneness with toothpick. Toothpick will come out clean when completely baked.

❖ Blueberry Muffin Tops ❖

1 c. GF bread flour mix (p. 13)
¼ tsp. Xanthan gum
1 tsp. baking powder
¼ tsp. vanilla powder or 1 tsp. GF vanilla
3 Tbsp.sugar
¼ tsp. salt
½ c. fresh or frozen blueberries
¼ tsp. cardamom
1 lg. egg
1 Tbsp. vegetable oil
~~1 tsp.~~ milk
1/2 C

Combine all dry ingredients in a medium size bowl. Mix egg, oil, milk, and blueberries. Add to dry ingredients.

Stir together, but do not over stir.

Divide mixture into 6 lightly buttered, or paper lined muffin cups.

Bake 350°, 12 minutes (muffin top pans) or 15 minutes (cupcake size).

Check for doneness with toothpick. Toothpick will come out clean when completely baked.

❖ Lemon Yogurt Poppy Seed ❖

1 c. GF Bread flour mix (p. 13)
¼ tsp. Xanthan gum
1 tsp. baking powder
¼ tsp. vanilla powder or 1 tsp. GF vanilla
3 Tbsp.sugar
¼ tsp. salt
1 6 oz carton lemon yogurt
½ tsp. lemon extract (GF)
1 lg. egg
1 Tbsp.vegetable oil
1 tsp. milk

Combine all dry ingredients in a medium size bowl. Mix egg, oil, milk, and lemon extract and yogurt. Add to dry ingredients.

Stir together, but do not over stir.

Divide mixture into 6 lightly buttered, or paper lined muffin cups.

Bake 350, 12 minutes (muffin top pans) or 15 minutes (cupcake size).

Check for doneness with toothpick. Toothpick will come out clean when completely baked.

Makes 6-8 muffins.

❖Miner's Pan Cake❖

3 eggs (separated)
1-½ c. GF bread flour mix (p.13)
½ tsp. Xanthan gum
3 Tbsp.sugar
½ tsp. salt
½ tsp. baking powder
¼ tsp. vanilla powder or 1 tsp. GF vanilla

Beat egg whites with electric mixer until almost stiff. Add egg yolks and sugar, mix well.

Fold in dry ingredients until blended. (Do not over-stir.)

Pour into an 8″ or 9″ buttered pie pan

Bake at 375° for 10 minutes.

Serves 4.

❖ Waffles ❖

1 c. GF bread flour mix (p. 13)
1 tsp. Xanthan gum
1 tsp. baking powder
¼ tsp. vanilla powder or 1 tsp. GF vanilla
2 Tbsp.sugar
½ tsp. salt
1 lg. egg
1 ½ Tbsp. vegetable oil
2/3 c. milk

Combine all dry ingredients; mix egg, oil and milk. Add to dry ingredients.

Stir until moistened. Do not over stir.

Pour ¼ cup per waffle square. Cook according to waffle maker directions.

Serve or freeze. These make great toaster waffles.

Makes 6 waffles.

❖ *Pancakes* ❖

1-c. GF bread flour mix (p. 13)
1 tsp. Xanthan gum
1 tsp. baking powder
¼ tsp. vanilla powder or 1 tsp. GF vanilla
2 Tbsp. sugar
½ tsp. salt
1 lg. egg
1 ½ Tbsp. vegetable oil
2/3 c. milk

Combine all dry ingredients; mix egg, oil and milk. Add to dry ingredients.

Stir until moistened. Do not over stir. Pour onto hot, lightly oiled, griddle or frying pan.

Makes 8-12 pancakes (depending on size).

5/10 – 2nd try used Toro Bread Mix Was tough!

❖ 10 Minute Cake Doughnuts ❖

V.G.

- 2 c. GF bread flour mix (p. 13)
- ~~2~~ 1/2 tsp. Xanthan gum
- 2 tsp. baking powder
- ½ tsp. salt
- 1/2 1 c. sugar
- ¼ tsp. nutmeg
- 1 c. half and half *used milk*
- 1 tsp. vanilla extract (or ¼ tsp. vanilla powder)
- 2 eggs

Added 1/4 c mashed potatoes (My mix + 1/2 c sorghum) Too moist! next day too dry — reheat 10 sec in microwave.

Preheat oven to 400°

Apply small amount of butter or vegetable oil to doughnut pans.

Mix dry ingredients in medium size mixing bowl. Stir in half and half, vanilla and eggs. Mix until moistened.

Do not spray donut maker – it burns

Spoon batter into prepared doughnut pans.

4 mins in Doughnut maker

Set timer for 10 minutes – remove from oven and cool on wire rack.

Shake doughnuts in a bag with ½ c. powdered (confectioner) sugar; fill with favorite jam or preserves.

Makes 1 dozen.

5/2010 – 1 1/2 c my mix + 1/2 c B. Red Mill cereal grain – ok but don't overmix!

❖ Apple Cobbler Crisp ❖

2 tart baking apples – peeled and sliced
1 Tbsp. butter (or GF margarine)
¼ c. brown sugar
½ tsp. cinnamon
1 c. GF bread flour mix (p. 13)
½ tsp. Xanthan gum
1 tsp. baking powder
½ tsp. salt
¼ c. granulated sugar
¼ c. milk or apple juice
1 lg. egg
1 tsp. vegetable oil
1 tsp. butter + 1 tsp. GF flour + 1 tsp. brown sugar (for topping)

In an 8"or 9" pie pan, spread butter, sprinkle with brown sugar and cinnamon. Placed sliced apple on top and bake in preheated 450°, hot oven (10-12 mins.)

While apple is baking; mix all dry ingredients and add milk or juice, egg and vegetable oil. Mix until moistened. Do not over stir.

Remove pan from oven; reduce oven temp to 350°. Pour batter over sizzling apples, top with mixture of butter, flour and brown sugar. Return to oven.

Continue baking for 10 –12 minutes or until golden and toothpick comes out clean.

Serves 6-8

Yummy with vanilla ice cream.

❖ Banana Bread ❖

1 c. GF bread flour mix (p. 13)
½ tsp. Xanthan gum
½ tsp. salt
1 tsp. baking powder
½ tsp. nutmeg
2 ripe bananas (mashed)
1 lg. egg
1 Tbsp. vegetable oil
1 Tbsp. water
Nuts optional

Preheat oven to 350°.

Combine all dry ingredients in medium bowl. Add mashed bananas, egg, oil and water. Mix until moistened. Do not over mix.

Pour into 1 lg. non stick (or buttered) loaf pan (or 2 small loaf pans).

Bake 30-35 minutes (small loaf pans), 50 –55 minutes (large loaf pan).

Test for doneness, with toothpick.

Cool on wire rack. Store in airtight containers or refrigerate.

Freezes well. Small loaves travel well too.

❖ Corn Bread or Corn Bread Muffins ❖

1 c. GF bread flour mix (p. 13)
¾ c. yellow corn meal
½ tsp. Xanthan gum
¼ c. sugar
½ tsp. salt
1 Tbsp. baking powder
1 egg (or substitute)
¼ c. vegetable oil
1 c. milk

Stir all dry ingredients together. Add egg, milk and oil. Stir until moistened (do not over stir.)

Pour into buttered (or non stick) 9x9" pan or 8 muffin cups, lined, buttered or non-stick.

Bake in hot 400° oven for 20-25 minutes. Bake muffins for 14-20 minutes.

If you are making this corn bread for breading or stuffing, turn off oven after baking and leave corn bread in oven for another half-hour.

❖ *Biscuits* ❖

1 ½ c. GF bread flour mix (p. 13)

2 tsp. baking powder

½ tsp. salt

1 tsp. Xanthan gum

½ c. milk

2 Tbsp. vegetable oil

1 egg, slightly beaten

mix + cut in 2 or 3 Tbsp butter

½

Were good!

Mix all dry ingredients. Add milk, egg and oil. Stir with spoon until mix is thick and holds together well.

Drop 6-8 heaping spoons onto cookie sheet. Bake 10 minutes *12 mins*

Or, flour cutting board with potato starch. Pat out dough to ½" thick. Cut with biscuit cutter. *Try this next time*

Preheat oven to 400°. Bake 10 minutes or until golden.

❖ Mustard Biscuits with Sesame Seeds ❖

1 ½ c. GF bread flour mix (p. 13)
2 tsp. baking powder
½ tsp. salt
1 tsp. Xanthan gum
½ c. milk
2 Tbsp. vegetable oil
1 egg, slightly beaten
1 tsp. dry mustard
1 Tbsp. sesame seeds

Mix all dry ingredients. Add milk, egg and oil. Stir with spoon until mix is thick and holds together well.

Drop 6-8 heaping spoons onto cookie sheet. Bake 10 minutes

Or flour cutting board with potato starch. Pat out dough to ½" thick. Cut with biscuit cutter.

Preheat oven to 400°. Bake 10 minutes or until golden. Top with sesame seeds.

❖ About Bread Crumbs ❖

Bread crumbs are little morsels of bread that can be used in a wide variety of dishes. The most common use for bread crumbs is as a coating for meat or vegetables that are going to be baked or fried. Bread crumbs do two things in this use, they help maintain moisture in the food and add a crunchiness.

Bread crumbs are used as fillers in meatloaves and toppings for casseroles. Used as filler, the bread crumbs add a lighter texture and when used on top of casseroles; color, eye appeal, texture and flavor.

Italian Bread Crumbs	**Corn Bread Crumbs**	**Devilishly Delicious Bread Crumbs**
1 c. bread crumbs 1 Tbsp. Italian seasoning 1 Tbsp. grated parmesan cheese	1 c. corn bread crumbs 1 tsp. chile powder ¼ tsp. black pepper *This is wonderful on egg casseroles.*	1 c. bread crumbs 1 tsp. dry mustard ¼ tsp. black pepper *This is a great breading for pork chops.*
Mix ingredients in a plastic bag, seal the bag and shake. Keep in freezer and use when needed.		

Basic bread crumbs can be gathered every time bread is cut. Crumbs can be made from the end cut of 3-5 day old bread and seasoned for any recipe. Generally corn bread and other breads should be stored in separate bags, and marked for easy identification.

Sharing a memory: My nephew, Kyle, was sitting on my lap at the dinner table. He was rubbing a cracker on the edge of the table. I asked; "What are you doing?" He replied, in his sweet 2-year-old voice; "Making crumbs".

Yeast Breads

Crowning White Bread

Dark Rye Bread

Golden Almond Bread Machine Method

Light Rye Bread Machine Method

Hamburger Buns/Sandwich Rolls/Baguettes

French Bread

Pizza Dough

❖ Crowning White Bread ❖

2 c. GF bread flour mix (p. 13)
1 ¾ teaspoons xanthan gum
½ tsp. salt
1 tsp. sugar
1 c. warm water
1 tsp. vinegar
3 Tbsp. melted butter
2 tsp. rapid rise yeast
2 large eggs

❖

Measure all dry ingredients into a large oven proof mixing bowl. Add water, eggs, vinegar and butter. Blend with spoon, then mix on high for 2 minutes. Batter will be cake like; moist and thick. Cover with a towel and let rise in a warm 150° oven or other warm spot, until doubled in size. With rapid rise yeast the first rise is about 30 minutes.

Return to mixer and beat on high for 2 minutes. Scrape batter into 1 large or 2 small loaf pans, non-stick. Place into warm oven to rise again (do not cover) until doubled. Heat oven to 350° and bake 30-35 minutes. Bread is done when golden and sounds hollow when tapped.

Remove from pan and cool on a wire rack.

This is an airy but moist bread, good for sandwiches on the first couple days. When it dries a little it makes wonderful French Toast.

Don't forget to save the crumbs for breaded meats

❖ Dark *Rye Bread ❖

2 c. GF bread flour mix (p. 13)
1 ¾ teaspoons xanthan gum
½ tsp. salt
¼ tsp. GF *rye flavor
1 Tbsp. dark molasses
1 c. warm water
1 tsp. vinegar
3 Tbsp. melted butter
2 tsp. rapid rise yeast
2 large eggs

❖

Measure all dry ingredients into a large oven proof-mixing bowl. Add water, molasses, eggs, vinegar and butter. Blend with spoon, then mix on high for 2 minutes. Batter will be cake like; moist and thick. Cover with a towel and let rise in a warm 150° oven or other warm spot, until doubled in size. With rapid rise yeast the first rise is about 30 minutes.

Return to mixer and beat on high for 2 minutes. Scrape batter into 1 large or 2 small non-stick loaf pans. Place into warm oven to rise again (do not cover) until doubled. Heat oven to 350° and bake 35-45 minutes (large loaf) 30-35 minutes (small loaves). Bread is done when dark brown and sounds hollow when tapped.

Remove from pan and cool on a wire rack.

This bread is versatile. The little loaves can be sliced thin, toasted in the broiler and used for open-faced snacks.

❖ Golden Almond Bread Machine Method ❖

1 2/3 c. GF bread flour mix (p. 13)
1 ¾ tsp. xanthan gum
2 Tbsp. almond meal
½ tsp. salt
1 tsp. sugar
1 c. warm water
1 tsp. vinegar
3 Tbsp. melted butter = ? cold
2 tsp. rapid rise yeast
2 large eggs

needs flavoring!

Add ingredients according to bread maker's directions.

Use White Bread setting; remove from bread maker when baking time is done.

Remove from pan and cool on a wire rack.

Almond meal adds color and texture.

– Used 1/3 c evap. milk + rest water
– 1 rounded tsp guar gum instead of xanthan
– The flour mix had few rice — I ended up adding about 1/2 c. or more rice + mix

Turned out too solid + moist, like store-bought.

❖ Light *Rye Bread Machine Method ❖

1 ¾ c. GF bread flour mix (p. 13)
1 ¾ teaspoons xanthan gum
½ tsp. salt
1 tsp. dark molasses
1 c. warm water
1 tsp. vinegar
3 Tbsp. melted butter
2 tsp. rapid rise yeast
2 large eggs
1 tsp. caraway seeds (optional)
¼ tsp. *rye flavor

Use bread machine directions for adding ingredients.

Set to White Bread. Bread maker will make an audible sound when done. Remove from bread maker.

Remove from pan and cool on a wire rack.

Start checking your bread about 10 minutes before finish time. It may be done early.

**Rye flavor manufactured by Authentic Foods. See Shopper's Guide (p.14).*

❖ Hamburger Buns/Sandwich Rolls/Baguettes ❖

2¼ c. bun mix (p. 13)
1 tsp. salt
1 Tbsp. sugar
1 ½ tsp. yeast (rapid rise)
2 lg. eggs, slightly beaten
3 Tbsp. butter, melted
1 c. warm water
1 tsp. vinegar

❖

Combine dry ingredients in a large, ovenproof bowl. Stir in wet ingredients. Mix on high for 2 minutes.

Place a towel over the bowl and place it in a warm place until doubled in bulk. About 30 minutes. A 150° oven works fine.

When doubled, return to mixer and beat on high for 2 minutes.

Divide batter into 6 muffin top pans and 2 parchment lined baguette pans.

Increase oven temperature to 350°. Bake 20-30 minutes, until bread is crusty and golden. Baguettes can need more time in the oven.

Remove from oven and cool on a wire rack.

Baguettes bake best on parchment cooking paper.

❖ French Bread ❖

2¼ c. bun mix (p. 13)
1 tsp. salt
1 Tbsp. sugar
1 ½ tsp. yeast (rapid rise)
1 lg. egg, slightly beaten
¼ c. plain yogurt
3 Tbsp. butter, melted
1 c. warm water
1 tsp. vinegar

❖

Combine dry ingredients in a large, ovenproof bowl. Stir in wet ingredients. Mix on high for 2 minutes.

Place a towel over the bowl and place it in a warm place until doubled in bulk. About 30 minutes. A 150° oven works fine.

When doubled, stir gently.

Pour batter into 2 parchment lined french bread molds or pans

Increase oven temperature to 350°. Bake 35-40 minutes, until bread is crusty and golden. Bread should sound hollow when tapped.

Remove from oven and cool on a wire rack.

Always line french bread pans with parchment, the crust gets brown and chewy.

❖ Pizza Dough ❖

3 c. pizza dough mix (p. 13)
½ tsp. salt
1 Tbsp. yeast (rapid rise)
2 Tbsp. sugar
1 ½ c. warm water
3 egg whites, slightly beaten
1 tsp. vinegar

❖

Mix all dry ingredients together in mixing bowl, add eggs, water and vinegar. Stir to moisten, beat on high speed, 2 minutes.

Batter will be soft and thick. Spread mixture onto non-stick pizza pans and let rise in warm oven (150°) until almost doubled, about 20 minutes.

When dough has doubled in size, increase oven temperature to 400° and bake for 12-15 minutes or until dough has shrunk away from the sides of the pans and slips off easily.

Cool on wire racks. Add pizza toppings of your choice and bake in hot 450° oven for 8-10 minutes or when toppings are bubbly.

See *how to do* photos (p. 110).

Alfredo sauce as a base pizza sauce is incredibly delicious!

Eggs & Other Breakfast Choices

Amelia's Deviled Eggs

Buckwheat Cereal

French Toast

Eggs Ole

Huevos Rancheros

Bread Pudding

Chile Relleno Casserole

Cranberry Orange Sticky Buns

Ham and Cheese Casserole

Seafood Omelet

Aebelskiver (Danish Pancakes)

❖ Amelia's Deviled Eggs ❖

6 hard cooked eggs
¼ c. GF mayonnaise
2 tsp. prepared mustard
1/8 tsp. celery salt
1/8 tsp. dill weed
paprika, to sprinkle on eggs

Peel eggs.

Slice in half.

Remove yolk.

Set aside egg whites.

In a small bowl, mix all ingredients except egg whites and paprika.

Stir with a wooden spoon. Spoon this mixture into the egg whites, sprinkle with paprika.

Makes 12 pieces.

These are Amelia's award winning eggs from 4-H.

❖ *Buckwheat Cereal* ❖

2 c. water
½ c. buckwheat (medium grain)
¼ c. dark molasses
½ c. raisins
½ c. milk
½ tsp. salt
½ tsp. pumpkin pie spice

Bring water, raisins and molasses to a boil, in a medium saucepan.

Add buckwheat, salt and spices. Cook on medium heat, stirring occasionally for about 8 minutes.

Stir in milk, reduce heat to low for a minute. Turn off heat and let rest for 5 minutes.

Serve with fresh fruit and milk.

Serves 2

This is delicious cold!

❖ French Toast ❖

8-pieces of (day old) bread, sliced ½-1 inch thick
1 ½ c. milk
2 eggs, slightly beaten
½ tsp. GF orange extract
¼ tsp. vanilla powder or 1 tsp. GF vanilla
¼ tsp. ground nutmeg
2 Tbsp. sugar

Place bread slices in a casserole dish 11x13. In a small bowl, mix all of the other ingredients. Pour ½ of the mixture over the bread, turn bread over and pour the remaining mix on top.

Let stand 20 minutes, to let the bread soak up all of the liquid.

Cook on a lightly oiled griddle, over medium-high heat, until lightly browned,

Serve with powdered sugar or syrup.

This freezes well and microwaves for a quick breakfast.

❖ Eggs Ole ❖

1 dozen eggs
1 large can, chopped mild chiles
1 c. Monterey Jack cheese shredded
1 c. mild cheddar cheese shredded
1 small can chopped ripe olives
1 dozen corn tortillas, cut into 2 inch wide strips (save ends cutts for topping)
Sour cream (optional)

❖

Preheat oven to 350

Cut tortillas, keep the end strips for topping, and line the bottom of a large casserole dish 11x13 inches.

Whip eggs in a large bowl; add chiles, Monterey Jack cheese, ½ cup cheddar cheese, and olives.

Pour half of the mixture over the tortillas. Place the rest of the tortilla strips on top; pour remaining egg mixture over tortillas and sprinkle with ½ cup cheddar cheese. Toss the tortilla ends on top.

Bake 25-30 minutes. Cheese should be slightly brown. Remove from oven and cool at least 10 minutes before cutting. Cut into squares and serve with a dollop of sour cream.

Serves 6-8

Great for brunch; serve with spicy refried beans and a mimosa (p. 174).

❖ Huevos Rancheros ❖

2 eggs and 2 tortillas, per person
Refried beans
Salsa, to taste
Sour cream, optional
Vegetable oil
Grated cheddar cheese

Lightly cook tortillas in hot vegetable oil. Place tortillas on broiler pan, (about 4 per pan) spread tortilla with a generous serving of beans. Lightly fry eggs, place egg on top of beans, sprinkle with cheese, top with salsa and broil until cheese is melted and eggs are cooked. Serve hot.

❖ Bread Pudding ❖

4 c. day old bread cubes
1 c. milk
1 egg
½ c. raisins
½ c. brown sugar
1 tsp. pumpkin pie spice
¼ tsp. vanilla powder or 1 tsp. GF vanilla

Mix milk, egg, raisins, brown sugar, vanilla, and pumpkin pie spice together in a 1½-qt. baking casserole dish. Add bread cubes, just to moisten.

Bake in a preheated 350° oven about 45 minutes. Pudding will be crunchy on top and moist inside. Spoon to serve.

Variations: add chopped dates, orange juice and dried cranberries or try chunks of pineapple.

❖ Chile Relleno Casserole ❖

1 lg. can mild green chiles (whole)
½ lb. Monterey Jack cheese, cut into strips to stuff chiles
1 c. cheddar cheese, grated
½ c. tortilla chips, crushed
½ c. corn bread crumbs (p. 36)
8 eggs, beaten

❖

Stuff chiles with strips of jack cheese, place on the bottom of a glass-baking dish 11x7x2.

Mix eggs, ½ cup cheddar cheese, tortilla bits, and bread crumbs. Pour over the top of the chiles.

Sprinkle remaining cheese on top.

Bake 350° for 35-40 minutes. Top will be golden and bubbly.

Remove from oven, cool 10 minutes before cutting.

Cut into squares and serve.

Serves 6-8.

This also makes a quick and meatless dinner dish.

To give this egg casserole a lift, add 1-teaspoon baking powder to the mix. The casserole will be almost an inch taller.

❖ Cranberry Orange Sticky Buns ❖

1 batch biscuits (p. 34)
1 tsp. orange zest, fresh
3 Tbsp. orange juice (frozen concentrated) thawed
2 Tbsp. brown sugar
½ c. dried cranberries
3 Tbsp. butter, softened
½ c. chopped nuts (optional)

❖

Heat oven to 350°.

Stir orange juice, brown sugar and cranberries in a small bowl, set aside.

Mix batch of biscuits, according to directions (p. 34) add orange zest.

Pour juice mixture into the bottom of an 8 or 9 inch round buttered baking pan.

Scoop large spoons full of the biscuit dough into the pan on top of the juice mix, continue until all biscuit dough has been used.

Bake 17-20 minutes. Remove from oven.

Place a larger plate over the pan and carefully invert biscuits onto the plate.

Serve now! These go fast.

If you want to try some other sticky stuff, here's my suggestion: spiced peaches with just a little extra brown sugar.

❖ Ham and Cheese Casserole ❖

8 lg. eggs
4 slices dry GF bread, cubed
1 c. Canadian bacon or ham (minced) (read ham labels for soy & wheat)
2 Tbsp. potato starch
2 tsp. baking powder
1 tsp. dry mustard
1 c. cheddar cheese, grated
1-c. cottage cheese (read label for modified food starch)
1 ½ c. water
Salt, pepper to taste

Beat eggs in a large mixing bowl. Add the rest of the ingredients.

Transfer mixture to an ovenproof, buttered, glass-baking dish 11x13.

Bake 350° for 35-40 mins. Until knife comes out clean when testing the center of the casserole.

Remove from oven, cool for about 10 minutes, cut into squares. Serve hot or cold.

Serves 6-8.

This can be made the night before, refrigerated and baked in the morning. Allow extra baking time. Reserve the baking powder and add just before baking.

❖ *Seafood Omelet* ❖

5 large eggs + 1 tsp. water, lightly whipped
1 Tbsp. butter
¼ c. cheddar cheese, grated
½ c. seafood, shrimp or crab meat
2 Tbsp. seafood sauce (optional)

❖

Heat butter on medium high heat in an 8 or 10 inch skillet, or omelet pan.

Pour eggs into pan. Eggs will begin to firm up in about a minute. With spatula, push eggs toward the center of the pan. **Liquid egg mixture will fill in where cooked egg has been pushed away.** Continue this until all egg is firm.

Sprinkle ½ of the seafood and most of the cheese onto the open omelet. Fold omelet in half. When cheese has melted, top with remaining seafood and serve.

5 egg omelet serves 2.

Fresh fruit of the season is a natural choice with this delicious omelet.

❖ Aebelskiver (Danish Pancakes) ❖

1 1/3 c. GF bread flour mix (p. 13)
1 tsp. xanthan gum
1/3 tsp. baking powder
1 c. milk
2 eggs (separated)
Powdered sugar for covering the aebelskiver

❖

You will need 3 bowls of varying sizes, 1 knitting needle #5 works well, and an aebelskiver pan.

If you don't have an aebelskiver pan, you can not make this!

Mix dry ingredients together in a medium size bowl. Mix milk and egg yolks in a small bowl. Beat egg whites until very light and fluffy, but not stiff.

Add milk and eggs to dry mixture, stir until all moist, fold egg whites into that mixture, stir until blended. Over-stirring makes the batter lose its airiness.

Heat aebelskiver pan over medium high heat and drop a smidgen of butter into each well. Pour batter into each well leaving about ¼ inch from the top.

(continued next page)

Aebelskiver (Danish Pancakes) Continued

When the batter starts to bubble and the sides start to look golden the aebelskiver should be ready to turn.

Insert a knitting needle into the batter and touch the inside of the well, try to move the little pancake with the needle. If the Aebelskiver is ready it will slip easily in the well. Lift until lower half of the ball is now on top. Continue cooking until center of ball is cooked.

Dust with powdered sugar, serve with chunky applesauce.

This looks like I wrote the instructions in Danish. It is easier than it looks.

Salads & Dressings

Spinach Salad

Coleslaw

South of the Border Salad

Grilled Chicken Caesar Salad

Pasta Spirals with Raspberry Dressing and Fruit

Cantaloupe & Curried Chicken Salad

Chinese Chicken Salad/ dressing

Croutons

Vegetable Pasta Salad

❖ Spinach Salad ❖

1 10-oz. package fresh spinach, or 2 fresh bunches
2 Tbsp. crumbled bacon (read the label)
5 or 6 mushrooms, sliced
½ purple onion, thinly sliced
2 hard cooked eggs, minced
1 c. croutons, (p. 67)

❖

In a large salad bowl, toss spinach with enough salad dressing to cover the spinach. Serve individual bowls with the dressed spinach and offer toppings in separate bowls.

Oil and Vinegar Dressing

¼ c. olive oil
½ c. red wine vinegar
½ tsp. sugar
1 Tbsp. water

Mix in a small bowl. Use as needed. This keeps, refrigerated, fresh for a long period of time.

Serves 4-6

❖ Coleslaw ❖

1 8-10 oz. package of coleslaw mix
½ c. GF mayonnaise
½ c. sour cream (read labels for modified food starch)
½ tsp. mustard powder
½ tsp. celery seeds
Salt and pepper to taste
1 Tbsp. vinegar
2 Tbsp. brown sugar

In a large bowl, mix brown sugar and vinegar; add mayonnaise, sour cream, mustard powder and celery seeds. Pour coleslaw mix into the sauce and toss. Salt and pepper to taste.

Serve or refrigerate immediately.

Optional additions: chopped apples, raisins, pineapple bits, chopped purple onions, or walnuts.

Serves 6-8.

❖ South of the Border ❖

1 large head of romaine lettuce
1 large or 2 medium oranges
1 small red onion
1 small can sliced olives

❖

Wash lettuce and shake dry. Remove the ribs. Slice the lettuce in ½ inch strips, horizontally.

Put cut lettuce into a large salad bowl.

Peel and slice the orange, separate the wedges, add to salad. Add olives and onions, toss and serve.

Oil and Vinegar Dressing

¼ c. olive oil
½ c. red wine vinegar
½ tsp. sugar
1 Tbsp. water
1 tsp. chile powder

Mix, in a small bowl, pour over entire salad just before serving.

Serves 6-8

❖ Grilled Chicken Caesar ❖

1 small head of romaine lettuce
1 grilled chicken breast
½ c. Caesar salad dressing (read the labels)
Parmesan Cheese
Croutons (p. 67)

Wash and pat dry lettuce break into pieces.

Divide into two large salad bowls.

Cube the chicken breast and toss onto lettuce.

Add salad dressing and toss gently. Sprinkle with parmesan and add croutons.

Serves 2.

This salad is awesome wrapped in a cold crêpe (p 166).

❖ Pasta Spirals with Raspberry Dressing and Fruit ❖

½ lb. rice spirals
1 c. grapes cut in half, seed removed
1 half pint blueberries
1 c. sliced strawberries
1 small can mandarin oranges, drained

❖

Cook rice spirals, according to package direction, drain and rinse.

Put pasta and fruit in a large bowl. Make dressing and toss.

Raspberry Dressing

1 c. plain yogurt
2 Tbsp. raspberry preserves
1 Tbsp. lemon juice

Mix in a small bowl, pour onto pasta salad

❖Cantaloupe & Curried Chicken Salad ❖

1 medium size cantaloupe
1 cooked chicken breast
2 Tbsp. capers
½ c. GF mayonnaise
½ c. sour cream or yogurt
Curry to taste
Salt and pepper to taste

Wash cantaloupe and slice in half. Remove the seeds. Use a melon ball scoop to get the melon out of the shell. Save the shell, it is the bowl.

Cube chicken breast, about ½ inch cubes.

Mix, in a medium size bowl, capers, mayonnaise and sour cream.

Add curry powder. Start with ½ tsp. curry, stir and taste. Adjust intensity of the curry to your taste.

Add cubed chicken and stir until all of the chicken is coated.

Put the melon balls back into the melon rinds, top with curried chicken salad. Serve with a warm baguette. (p. 42)

❖ Chinese Chicken Salad/ Dressing ❖

1 chicken breast, broiled or baked
2 c. mixed salad greens
4-6 mushrooms, sliced
2 c. rice threads, cooked

❖

Cut chicken breast into long thin strips, then cut in half so pieces are about 2-1/2 inches.

Slice mushrooms. Chop rice threads several times.

Divide salad mix into two large salad bowls. Top with chicken, mushrooms and rice threads.

Dressing for Chinese Chicken Salad

½ c. seasoned rice vinegar
¼ c. GF soy sauce (most soy sauces contain wheat)
¼ c. water
2 Tbsp. vegetable oil
1 tsp. sugar

Mix in a small bowl. Spoon dressing over individual salad.

Serves 2

❖ Croutons ❖

Heat oven to 200°.

Use any day old bread, or older.

Cut into bite size cubes. Place on cookie sheet so there is lots of room to toast individually.

Bake 20 minutes, turn croutons over with a spatula. Repeat this 2 more times. (1 hour process) Remove from oven and cool on cookie sheet.

While still warm, prepare seasoning in a self-seal plastic bag, add croutons and shake.

Seal and store in refrigerator, these can be toasted again in a hot skillet before serving.

Time saving hint: Save bread in freezer, make a couple batches of croutons at the same time.

Seasoning ideas: Italian seasoning, and parmesan cracked pepper and celery salt.

❖ Vegetable Pasta Salad ❖

½ lb. rice spirals, vegetable flavored and colored
1 c. cherry tomatoes
1 bell pepper, julienne style
1 c. carrots, baby, or cut into coins
1 lg. can ripe olives, drained
1 bunch green onions, sliced

❖

Cook pasta according to directions on the package. (No salt), drain and rinse.

Wash and cut all vegetables. In a large mixing bowl, toss pasta and vegetables with the dressing.

Dressing for Vegetable Pasta

¼ c. vegetable oil
1 Tbsp. capers
½ c. red wine vinegar
½ tsp. oregano
¼ c. water

Mix in small bowl.

Soups

Cream of Celery Soup

Cream of Chicken Soup

Cream of Mushroom Soup

Pasta y Frigoli – Italian Lentil Soup with Pasta

French Onion Soup

12 Minute Cream of Tomato Soup

❖ Cream of Celery Soup ❖

3 large ribs of celery, minced
1 large white onion, minced
1 ½ c. water
2 tsp. chicken base
½ c. heavy cream
2 Tbsp. potato starch & ½ c. water dissolved together
1 Tbsp. butter

Melt butter in a medium saucepan. Sauté onions and celery until onions are tender.

Add water and chicken base, turn heat to high. Bring to a boil. Add cream and potato starch water. Continue cooking, stirring constantly until soup thickens.

Serve hot or cool and freeze.

Yield: 3 ½ c.

This soup base is a product I know to be GF. Better than Bullion by Superior Touch, by Superior Quality Foods – found in the soup section of most major markets. Refrigerate after opening (each jar makes 41 servings). Varieties: chicken & beef.

❖ Cream of Chicken Soup ❖

2 c. cubed cooked chicken
½ tsp. paprika
1 large rib of celery, minced
1 large white onion, minced
1 ½ c. water
2 tsp. chicken base
½ c. heavy cream
2 Tbsp. potato starch & ½ c. water dissolved together
1 Tbsp. butter

Heat butter in a medium saucepan. Sauté onion and celery until onion is tender.

Add water and chicken base, turn heat to high. Bring to a boil. Add cream and potato starch water. Continue cooking, stirring constantly until soup thickens.

Serve now or freeze.

Serves 4

This soup base is a product I know to be GF. Better than Bullion by Superior Touch, by Superior Quality Foods – found in the soup section of most major markets. Refrigerate after opening (each jar makes 41 servings). Varieties: chicken and beef.

❖ Cream of Mushroom Soup ❖

8 oz. Fresh mushrooms, minced
2 cloves garlic, minced
1 large yellow onion, minced
2 c. of half and half or 1 c. milk and 1 c. heavy cream
2 Tbsp. potato starch & ½ c. of water dissolved together
½ c. cream sherry
1 Tbsp. butter
Salt & pepper to taste

Melt butter in medium saucepan. Add onions, mushrooms and garlic. Sauté until onion is soft.

Add half and half, stirring constantly until mixture comes to a boil. Add potato starch water, stir until thickened. Turn stove off, add cream sherry and stir.

Serve immediately or freeze for future use.

Makes 3 ½ c.

❖ Pasta y Frigoli – Italian Lentil Soup with Pasta ❖

2 c. dry lentils rinsed and soaked 2 hours.
6 lean sliced of bacon (minced)
1 onion chopped
2 stalks celery sliced
3 cloves garlic chopped
1 quart of water
2 cans finely cut tomatoes
1 can kidney beans drained
½ lb. rice pasta (cooked to package instructions)
1 bay leaf (optional)

Sauté bacon bits in the large soup pot. Add onion, celery, garlic, tomatoes, lentils and 1 quart of water. Simmer about 2 hours.

When lentils are tender to the bite, or al dente, add cooked pasta and kidney beans.

Because this recipe is so large, it can be divided and parts frozen before adding pasta **(rice pasta does not freeze well!)**

Serves 8-10

❖ French Onion Soup ❖

2 large yellow onions, sliced julienne style
2 tsp. beef bullion base
2 c. water
2 slices swiss cheese
Toasted GF bread wafers
Sprinkle of nutmeg (optional)

❖

Caramelize onions in hot saucepan. When onions are brown add water and beef base.

Ladle into 2 ovenproof bowls, top with toast wafers & Swiss cheese. Put into hot oven 400° until cheese melts.

Serve immediately.

Serves 2

This recipe multiplies easily up to 6 servings.

If making for a crowd, caramelize onions overnight in a slow cooker.

This soup base is a product I know to be GF. Better than Bullion by Superior Touch, by Superior Quality Foods – found in the soup section of most major markets. Refrigerate after opening (it seems a little expensive but each jar makes 41 servings). Varieties: chicken & beef.

❖ 12 Minute Cream of Tomato Soup ❖

(10 minutes, without onions)

2 c. canned, crushed tomatoes
1 large onion-minced
½ tsp. baking soda
2 c. milk
2 Tbsp. butter
2 Tbsp. potato starch dissolved in
¼ c. water

In a large saucepan, sauté onions in butter until they are tender. Add tomatoes and bring to boiling.

Remove from heat; add baking soda, stir until dissolved, stir in milk, return to stove, continue stirring until soup comes to a boil. Add the potato starch water, stir until thickened.

Return to heat and cook on medium until the soup is heated through.

Yield 3-4 servings (1 qt.).

Serve now, with a grilled cheese sandwich!

Freeze in 1-c. units for later use.

Sandwiches

Ham and Cheese Sub

Tuna Salad for Sandwiches

Egg Salad

Salmon Salad

*Pastrami on *Rye*

Peanut Butter and Jelly

❖ *Ham and Cheese Sub* ❖

1 whole baguette (p. 42)
3 slices deli ham (no soy sauce enhancer)
2 Swiss or cheddar cheese slices
GF mayonnaise
Mustard (Dijon style)
Lettuce
Tomato

Slice foot long baguette in half lengthwise, spread with mayonnaise and mustard. Stack ham, cheese, lettuce and tomato. Cut sandwich in two 6 inch sandwiches.

Serves 2

❖ Tuna Salad for Sandwiches ❖

8 oz. white tuna, water packed
2 Tbsp. of GF mayonnaise
½ tsp. dill weed
½ c. cheddar cheese, cubed (small cubes)
dill pickle, red onion, lettuce, tomato, sprouts, cucumber (optional)

Drain tuna and break apart in small mixing bowl, add mayonnaise, dill weed and cheese.

Slice 2 sandwich buns (p. 42)

or 1 baguette (p. 42)

Pile tuna salad onto bun; add your favorite sandwich toppings.

Makes 2 servings

❖ Egg Salad ❖

4 hard cooked eggs, chopped
3 Tbsp. GF mayonnaise
¼ tsp. salt
½ tsp. horseradish (optional)
Pepper to taste

Put chopped eggs, mayonnaise, salt and pepper in a small mixing bowl. Stir.

Spread on toasted *rye bread (p. 39 or 41) Cut into triangles.

Serve open-faced.

Makes 2 servings

❖ Salmon Salad ❖

1 large can pink salmon drained and boned or 2 c. fresh cooked
½ c. plain yogurt
1 tsp. lemon juice
½ c. celery, chopped
1 small can chopped ripe olives (optional)

Mix all ingredients in a small bowl.
Serving suggestions:

*Artichoke filled with salmon salad

*In a bed of lettuce

*On a sandwich.....now that you have some good recipes to make some good breads.

*Or with those yummy cheese and flax crackers (p. 177)

❖ Pastrami on *Rye ❖

2 slices *rye bread (p. 39 or 41)
4 slices deli pastrami (read the label)
2 slices Swiss cheese
Mustard (sake-wasabi)
Mayonnaise
Lettuce (red leaf or romaine)
Tomato, sliced
Avocado, sliced

Slice *rye bread in ½" slices, spread with mayonnaise and mustard. Pile on pastrami, swiss cheese, lettuce tomato and avocado.

This makes a wonderful grilled pastrami sandwich too. Don't add lettuce, tomato and avocado before cooking.

❖ *Peanut Butter and Jelly* ❖

Peanut Butter

Jelly

GF Bread (p. 38-43)

Assemble sandwich.

There are plenty of good GF peanut butters on grocery store shelves, some fresh peanut butters in specialty stores and made-to-order in health food stores.

There are jellies without artificial colors but a better selection of GF spreads will be in fruit preserves, jams and fruit butters.

*There are loads of good recipes for homemade jams and preserves...**just not in this book**.*

Cooking Instructions for Asian Noodles

Cooking instructions, on Asian noodle packages, are interesting. The translations are different on each type of noodle but the graphics are pretty darned good. Some depict the pot boiling and the noodles going in and continue to boil. Some show little clocks so you know how much time it takes. And they also show how to use the noodle in different recipes.

With the flat rice noodles, there are limited instructions, mostly not in English. So, here is my spin on the flat, rice noodle. Bring lots of water to a rolling boil, add noodles, turn heat off, cover pan and let stand for about 6 minutes or until the noodle is almost white and is al dente.

Remember, never salt rice noodles or rice pasta.

Pastas

Introduction to Pastas

3 Cheese Macaroni Bake

Pasta Pizza Salad

Spinach Stuffed Lasagna Rolls

Lasagna with Meat Sauce

Spaghetti and Meatballs

Lemon Linguini

Spaghetti All'uova or Poor Man's Spaghetti

Crab & Shrimp Seashell Pasta Salad

Introduction to Pastas

Photo on page 108 shows some of the varieties that are not made with wheat.

Most of the pastas shown there are made with rice, some with bean and some with corn.

In most of the Asian (Thai, Korean, Japanese and Chinese) recipes, a noodle or two might be called for.

Rice Noodles

Most larger supermarkets, throughout America, have an Oriental section with a limited selection of rice noodles. The best selections will be found in larger cities in oriental markets. *I always stock up my noodle supply in these stores.*

Rice Pastas

We now have a wonderful selection of commonly used pasta shapes, manufactured by at least three Canadian firms. *Thank you Canada.*

These pastas are made from brown rice, brown rice and rice bran, and white rice. The texture and color of this pasta is comparable to wheat pasta. Rice pastas can be found in specialty food stores and in most health food stores.

Corn Pastas

While corn pasta is limited, health food stores carry packaged products and larger health food stores sell it in bulk. Corn pasta does not have the texture of wheat pasta and it is quite yellow.

Other wheat and gluten free pastas are made with bean flour and potato flour. I had no success with these pastas, so I stick with the tried and true foods. This is merely the opinion of the author.

Home Made

There are many recipes for GF pasta. My favorite is made with cornstarch, potato starch and tapioca starch. Making home made pasta is fun and easy to do. I use a pasta machine technique when making manicotti or ravioli. This recipe for fresh pasta can be found in Bette Hagman's, "More from the Gluten Free Gourmet" page 228. *Thanks Bette.*

Pasta Shapes

Pasta is shaped for a purpose in its use. The best example is lasagna.

The ridges and twists in some pasta are to catch the sauce. The wideness of fettuccini and the thinness of spaghetti have their purpose in the meal. Right now, we're not going for ambiance; we're going for availability. Here's what is in the stores now.

Ener-G Foods, Pastariso and Tinkyada. (In alphabetical order) These fine manufacturers make lasagna, penne, fussili, shells, macaroni, linguini, fettuccini, spaghetti, spirals and other shapes.

Mrs. Leepers is now making alphabets and zoo animal rice pastas for kids. This product is made in California, U.S.A.

These products can be found in most health food stores, even small stores can special order for you.

Helpful Hints for Cooking and Using Rice Pasta

- **No Salt**, it breaks down the pasta to mush!
- **Do not overcook,** al dente is perfect for serving right away, undercooking is best if you use the pasta in soups or casseroles
- **Do not freeze,** same as salt, the pasta breaks down. Lasagna is the exception to this rule.

❖ 3 Cheese Macaroni Bake ❖

½ lb. rice macaroni
1 c. cheddar cheese, grated
1 c. Monterey jack cheese, grated
1 c. cottage cheese
Salt and pepper to taste

Cook macaroni according to package instructions (no salt) drain and rinse.

In an ovenproof 2-qt. Deep-dish casserole mix cheeses together. Add macaroni, stirring gently until all pasta has been covered. Sprinkle with pepper.

Bake, 350° for 20 minutes remove from oven and stir, Return to oven for 20-25 minutes and the top is golden brown.

Serves 6

Serve with a large spinach salad.

❖ Pasta Pizza Salad ❖

½ lb. rice spirals
2 medium tomatoes, peeled, seeded and chopped
1 /2 lb. hot pepper cheese, cubed
4-5 green onions, sliced thinly
1 stick pepperoni, sliced (**Hormel® brand, says Gluten Free on the label**)
½ c. light olive oil
¼ c. red wine vinegar
1 tsp. Italian seasoning
½ tsp. garlic salt
Salt and pepper to taste
1/3 c. grated parmesan cheese

Cook pasta according to package directions (no salt), drain and rinse.

In a small bowl, combine oil, wine vinegar, spices and parmesan cheese.

In a large bowl, combine pasta, tomatoes, hot pepper cheese, onions and pepperoni. Pour oil and vinegar mixture over the pasta. Refrigerate for a couple hours and add more salt and pepper if needed.

To add more color and texture add, sliced olives, sliced mushrooms, and sliced bell pepper.

❖ Spinach Stuffed Lasagna Rolls ❖

8 rice lasagna noodles
1 c. frozen chopped, or 1 c. fresh (cooked and chopped)
1 c. ricotta cheese
½ c. parmesan cheese, grated
1 c. mozzarella cheese, grated
2 c. marinara sauce (p. 21)

Cook lasagna according to package directions (no salt), drain and rinse.

Mix cheeses and spinach; spread evenly on lasagna noodles. Roll each noodle and place, seam side down, on 11x13 baking dish.

Bake 350° 20-25 mins. until cheese is melted. Pour heated marinara sauce over noodles, sprinkle with parmesan or mozarella cheese, and return to oven for 5 minutes.

Serves 8

One per person is very satisfying! Lasagna noodles can be frozen!

❖ Lasagna with Meat Sauce ❖

9 lasagna noodles
1 batch lasagna sauce (p. 19) or your favorite lasagna sauce
1 c. ricotta cheese
16 oz. mozzarella cheese, grated
½ c. parmesan cheese

❖

Cook noodles according to package directions (no salt).

Stir parmesan cheese into ricotta cheese.

Ladle sauce onto the bottom of an 11x13-casserole dish. Place 3 noodles on the sauce. Ladle more sauce over the noodles. Spoon on 1/2 ricotta mix and sprinkle on mozzarella. Repeat this step. Place the last 3 noodles on top, cover with sauce and spread the remaining mozzarella on top.

Bake 350° for 40-45 minutes. Top will be golden and bubbly. Remove from oven and let stand 10 minutes before cutting. Cut into squares and serve.

Prepare 2 casseroles, bake one, freeze one.

You deserve a glass of wine. Get it!

❖ *Spaghetti and Meatballs* ❖

1 8 oz. package rice spaghetti or oriental rice vermicelli
1 batch meat loaf mix (p. 131)
1 batch Marinara sauce (p. 21) or favorite spaghetti sauce

❖

Cook pasta according to package directions. (no salt), rinse and drain

Mix meatloaf according to recipe and add garlic and spices. Form into bite sized balls, about 50 of the little darlings, place on a large cookie sheet and bake 350° for about 20 minutes. Remove from oven and spoon onto a plate.

Simmer marinara sauce while the meatballs are baking.

5 meatballs per serving is a good rule of thumb. Put as many as you need into the sauce. Continue simmering until ready to serve.

To reheat the drained spaghetti, pour boiling water over it. This also loosens the noodles. Dish individual portions right from the stove onto the plate. Sprinkle with parmesan cheese and serve.

These meatballs are light and moist. They freeze well in a freezer bag.

Great meatball sandwiches! *(See color photos page 100)*

❖ Lemon Linguini ❖

½ lb. rice linguini noodles or ¼ inch flat oriental rice noodles
3 Tbsp. butter
1 can tomatoes, chopped
¼ c. lemon juice
1 tsp. lemon zest

Cook linguini to directions on package, (no salt) drain and rinse.

In a large skillet, melt butter; add lemon juice, zest and tomatoes. Heat until bubbly, but not boiling. Add linguini and heat completely before serving.

Light, easy and unbelievably delicious.

Serves 4-6

❖ Spaghetti All'uova or Poor Man's Spaghetti ❖

½ lb. rice spaghetti pasta, or Oriental rice vermicelli
1 Tbsp. romano or parmesan cheese
3 eggs
3 Tbsp. butter

Cook pasta to the directions on the package, (no salt), drain and rinse.

In a medium hot wok, or other large frying pan, melt butter, add drained spaghetti. Stir until hot.

In a small bowl; beat eggs, add cheese. Pour egg mixture over spaghetti. Cook until eggs set. Serve at once.

Serves 4-6

"The Old World Traditional" method was to pour un-rinsed, hot pasta over the eggs, at the table and serve.

Crab and Shrimp Sea Shell Pasta Salad

2-6 oz. cans crab meat
6 oz. shrimp, frozen and defrosted
¼ c. red pepper, chopped
2/3 c. sour cream
2/3 c. GF mayonnaise
½ lb. rice shells
1 tsp. dill weed
1 small can sliced olives
½ c. chopped celery
1 tsp. dry mustard

Cook rice shell pasta to directions on package. Drain and rinse.

Pour pasta into a large mixing bowl.

Mix all of the rest of the ingredients and pour over pasta.

Eat now or let salad chill in refrigerate for a few hours.

This is the "cover salad," it was my mom's recipe and only fixed for special occasions.

IT'S ALL IN THE PAN

The key to **successful** baking is the right pan and a good recipe. Now all you need is the pan!

10 Minute Doughnuts (p. 28)

BREAKFAST
in minutes

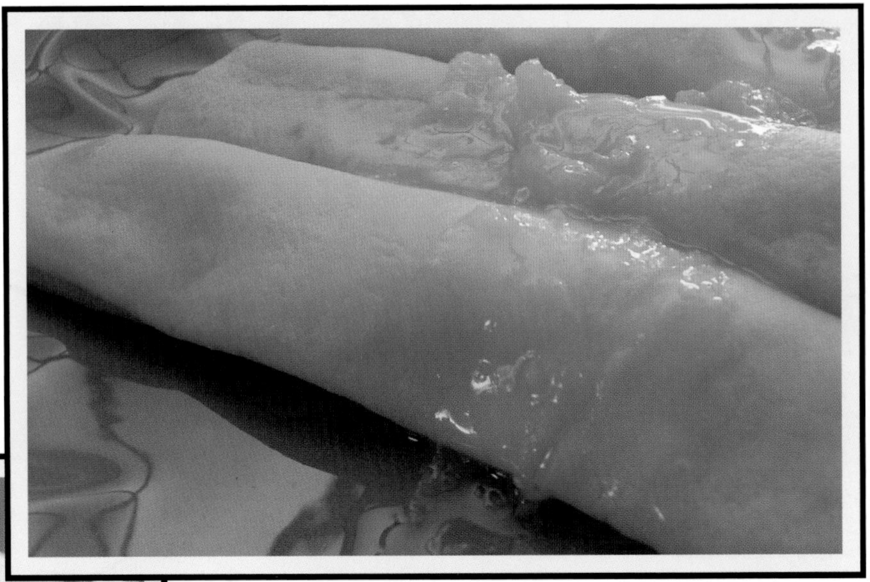

Orange Crêpes (p. 166-167)

Hot Buckwheat Cereal (Kasha)

Apple Mini Bundt Cakes (p.151)

Top left: Cranberry Orange Sticky Buns (p. 53)

Left: Waffles (p. 28)

Above right: 10 Minute Doughnuts (p. 30)

LUNCH &

Hearty Lentil Soup - pasta y frigoli (p. 73)

Buckwheat Thins (p. 178)

Foot-long Meatball Sub

Meatballs (p. 93)

Baguette (p. 42)

DINNER ... *times to savor*

Stuffed Bell
Peppers and
Creamy Tomato Soup

Dilled Baked Salmon and Fettuccini Alfredo

COOKIES & BARS

Brownies (p. 159)

No Flour Peanut Butter Chocolate Chip Cookies (p158)

Coconut Macaroons (p. 161)

CAKES

Morro
Rock
Cake
(p. 150)

Carrot Cake (p. 152)
with
Cream Cheese Icing

Pans that Shape Bread

Classic French Loaf Pans Bread

Baguettes

Mini loaf pans

Banana Bread (p. 32)

It is far **cheaper** to buy one good pan every week than to buy one loaf of bread you can't eat.

Basic Pans for Basic Breads

- Mini loaves
- 1 lb. loaf pans
- Cookie sheets
- Rounds
- Squares
- Casseroles in varying sizes
- Muffin pans, muffin tops & mini muffins
- Doughnut pans
- Waffle maker

Muffin Top Pans

Sandwich Rolls

Use you baking equipment exclusively for your Gluten Free foods. **Avoid cross contamination**

BREAD MAKING TECHNIQUES

- **Bread machines take a longer time but are not as labor intensive.**
  1 loaf in 2 hours 40 minutes
- **Oven Method is so quick with GF batter.**
  4 loaves in just 1 hour.

Bread Machine ←

Oven Baked ←

Bread Machine Light *Rye (p. 41)

Oven Baked Crowning White (p. 38)

Bread Flour mix (p. 13)

Sandwiches begin with bread

Pastrami on *Rye (p. 82)

Ham and Cheese Sub (p. 78)
Dill Pickles (p. 120)

Hamburger Buns (p. 42)
Oven Fries (p. 121)

PASTAS

Wide Rice Noodles
Bean Threads
Penne
Macaroni
Fussilli
Spirals
Lasagna
Rice Shells
Vegetable Spirals
Rice Threads
Rice Vermicelli
Corn Pagodas
Alphabets
Brown Rice Spirals
Vegetable Zoo Shapes

Pasta Shapes

RICE

Pastas

Top: Lasagna

Left: Spinach Stuffed Lasagna Noodles & Marinara Sauce

Right: Fusilli with Meat Sauce

PIZZA *step by step*

1) Mix (left)

2) Spread (above)

3) Bake & Cool (right)

Pepperoni Pizza

Complete Directions on Page 44

To Your Good Health

Seafood Omelet (p. 55)

Peanut Butter & Jelly Sandwich (p. 83)

Baguettes & Buns (p. 42)

Lemon Poppy Seed (p. 26) & Blueberry Muffins (p. 25)

Potato & Rice Dishes

Risotto

Twice Baked Potatoes with Zip

San Diego Mashed Potatoes

Creamy Potatoes and Broccoli Bake

Two-timing Rice and Potatoes

Garlic Mashed Potatoes

Dilled Potato Salad

Potato Wedges

Scalloped Potatoes

Sour Cream and Onion Bake

❖ Risotto ❖

3 Tbsp. butter
1 medium onion, chopped
1 c. long grain white rice
3 c. water
3 tsp. chicken base* (GF)
½ c. cheddar cheese, grated
½ c. Monterey Jack cheese, grated
Saffron tea

Melt butter in saucepan, sauté onion until tender. Add rice, cook for 2 minutes. Pour in water and chicken soup base. Cook until almost all of the broth is gone, about 1 hour. Add saffron tea and cheese; cook to desired thickness, 30-45 minutes.

Make saffron tea: Add 1 pinch saffron to 1 c. boiling water. Let the tea steep for at least ½ hour.

*Chicken base: GF Superior Foods chicken base is found in the soup section of larger markets.

❖ Twice Baked Potatoes with Zip ❖

4 baking potatoes
4 Tbsp. butter
½ c. milk
½ c. hot pepper cheese, grated

Scrub potatoes, and prick air holes on the top. Bake in 350° oven for 45 minutes or soft to the touch. Remove from oven.

Cut in half, lengthwise. Scoop out cooked potato into a mixing bowl.

Reserve potato skin to fill again.

Add butter to cooked potato and mash with fork or potato masher, whip in milk continue until potatoes are smooth.

Spoon mashed potatoes back into the potato skins, top with grated pepper cheese. Return to hot oven for 10 minutes and cheese is melted.

❖ San Diego Mashed Potatoes ❖

10 large potatoes, peeled and cubed
½ c. boiling water
½ c. heavy cream
salt and pepper to taste

Cook potatoes in a large pot, with enough water to cover them. When potatoes are tender, but not mushy, remove from heat and drain.

With electric mixer beat the potatoes slowly while adding boiling water, beat on high until potatoes are very airy and smooth. Add cream and whip until potatoes are fluffy. Serve immediately.

These remarkably easy potatoes are remarkably tasty.

❖ *Creamy Potatoes and Broccoli Bake* ❖

10 medium red potatoes
1 c. cream of celery soup (p. 76)
1 bunch of broccoli, broken into flowerets

Wash potatoes, poke holes in the potato with a fork.

Put potatoes in a medium 3 qt. flat casserole dish. Bake 350° for 30 minutes. Remove from oven.

Steam broccoli for 4 minutes; remove from heat and drain.

Put steamed broccoli in with the potatoes, fitting the broccoli in between the potatoes. Cover with cream of celery soup. Return to the oven cooking another 15 minutes, or potatoes are tender and soup is bubbly.

This is especially good with baked chicken.

❖ Two-timing Rice and Potatoes ❖

1 c. leftover rice
2 c. leftover mashed potatoes
¼ c. parmesan cheese

Butter a small frying pan; mix rice and potatoes together. Sprinkle with parmesan cheese, cover and stir occasionally. Cook about 20 minutes

Believe it or not, this is good!

❖ Garlic Mashed Potatoes ❖

6 large russet potatoes, or any other baking potato.
Water to cover potatoes
1 tsp. salt
6 cloves garlic
½ c. milk
3 Tbsp. butter

Peel and cube potatoes. In a large saucepan, cook potatoes, on high until boiling. When water boils, add garlic. Continue cooking until potatoes are tender. Remove from heat and mash. Add butter and milk, whipping until potatoes are smooth.

This is so robust it is a great side dish for BBQ steak.

❖ Dilled Potato Salad ❖

8-10 medium red potatoes
4 hard cooked eggs, chopped
1 c. GF mayonnaise
1 c. sour cream
2 Tbsp. prepared mustard
1 heaping teaspoon dill weed, dried
1 c. dill pickle, chopped (optional) (p. 181)
Salt and pepper to taste

❖

Wash and cut potatoes into about ½ inch cubes. Cook potatoes in a large pot, add enough water to cover potatoes. Cook, medium heat, until tender.

Drain potatoes in a colander, rinse in cold water, and chill.

While potatoes are cooling, mix, in a large bowl, eggs, mayonnaise, sour cream, mustard and dill weed together. Add chopped pickles.

Add chilled potatoes. Cover and refrigerate for an hour or more. Taste, and add salt and pepper if needed.

Chilling tip: Pour potatoes onto a wax paper lined cookie sheet. Place cookie sheet into the freezer for 10 minutes.

❖ Potato Wedges ❖

1 large russet potato, per person
Chile powder
Salt
Pepper
Olive oil

Heat oven to 400°.

Scrub potatoes, cut into wedges about 1 inch wide.

Lightly oil the bottom of a baking pan (whatever size to fit your needs).

Place potato wedges in the pan, skin side down. Sprinkle with salt, pepper and chile (to taste).

Bake about 20 minutes, until tender and browned.

Serve with sour cream and chives.

❖ Scalloped Potatoes ❖

4 lg. potatoes
1 lg. yellow onion, sliced julienne style
1 Tbsp. vegetable oil
½ c. ricotta or cottage cheese
½ c. cheddar cheese

Over a moderate heat, sauté onions in a lightly oiled 10-inch frying pan.

Wash and slice potatoes into ¼ inch coins. Stir potatoes in with the onions. Cover and simmer for about 20 minutes, stirring occasionally. When potatoes are tender stir in ricotta cheese and sprinkle cheddar cheese over the top. Cover and simmer for 5 minutes.

This is a hearty side dish with eggs at camp!

❖ Sour Cream and Onion Bake ❖

3 large onions, sliced in rings
5 potatoes, peeled and cubed
½ c. water
1 c. sour cream
¼ c. chunky salsa

Heat oven to 350°.

Mix onion, potatoes and water in a covered 3-qt. Baking dish. Bake for 25 minutes.

Remove from oven; add sour cream and salsa. Return to oven, bake until sour cream is bubbly and potatoes are tender, about 15 minutes.

Main Dishes

Swiss Steak Bake
Stuffed Peppers
Deviled Pork Chops
Baked Salmon in Dill Sauce
Italian Sausage Stuffed Mushrooms
Basic Meatloaf
Meat and Bean Burritos
Chicken Florentine
San Luis Obispo Chicken Chile Relleno
Green Chile Chicken
Pork Roast and Gravy
Fish and Chips
Eggplant Parmesan
Slow Cook-Corned Beef Dinner
Beef Stroganoff
Shrimp and Fish Au Gratin

❖ Swiss Steak Bake ❖

1 2 lb. sirloin steak cut into thin strips
1/3 c. potato starch
1 tsp. salt
2 tsp. pepper
3 Tbsp. molasses
3 Tbsp. GF Soy Sauce (**most soy sauces contain wheat**)
1 medium red pepper cubed
1 medium onion sliced julienne style
1 c. celery, sliced

Mix potato starch, salt and pepper in flat bowl. Lightly coat meat strips.

In a lightly oiled hot wok brown the meat.

Put browned meat into a 2 qt. casserole. Add soy sauce, molasses and fresh vegetables. Mix well.

Bake at 300° covered for 25-30 minutes or meat and vegetables tender.

Serves 4

❖ Stuffed Peppers ❖

1 lb. ground round or hamburger
2 tsp. salt
2 tsp. pepper
1 tsp. ground chile powder
1 c. cooked rice
2 c. creamy tomato soup (p.75)
3 large bell peppers, red, green, yellow or orange

Brown meat in frying pan or wok. Drain and return to pan.

Season meat with salt, pepper and chile powder. Add cooked rice.

Wash and seed peppers. Stuff with rice and meat. Set pepper tops on top and hold with toothpicks (3 each).

Place peppers in your smallest pot so peppers stay upright when steaming.

Steam in about 2 c. water for about 20 minutes, just until pepper is al dente.

Heat creamy tomato soup.

Remove peppers from pot onto plate. Ladle hot soup over opened peppers.

Prep time 20 minutes, cook time 20 minutes.

Serves 2-3

❖ Deviled Pork Chops ❖

4 boneless pork chops ½ inch thick
1 c. potato starch
2 tsp. dry mustard
¼ tsp. pepper
1 tsp. salt
2 Tbsp. Olive oil
1 ½ c. water
4 medium red potatoes
1 large onion sliced, julienne style
2 carrots sliced into ¼ inch coins

❖

Mix potato starch, salt and pepper in flat bowl. Lightly coat pork chops in mixture (keep excess flour mixture for thickening gravy).

Heat oil in a hot frying pan. Brown both sides of pork chops quickly and remove from pan, set aside.

Add 1 c. water to pan and bring to boil. Turn heat down when it begins to boil.

Mix ¼ c. water with remaining flour mixture. Add to pan stirring constantly until gravy thickness.

Put chops, potatoes, onions and carrot coins into gravy. Cook on medium heat until potatoes are tender, about 40 minutes.

Serves 4

❖ Baked Salmon in Dill Sauce ❖

1 two lb. boneless salmon filet
4 Tbsp. GF dill sauce or 4 Tbsp. homemade dill sauce (below)

❖

Place filet in a glass-baking dish, skin side down.
Baste with dill sauce.
Bake uncovered, 30 minutes, 350° Oven
Serve hot or cold
Serve 3-4

Homemade Dill Sauce

3 Tbsp. plain yogurt
1 Tbsp. fresh lemon juice
1 tsp. Dill weed, dry or fresh
Mix in small bowl

❖ Italian Sausage Stuffed Mushrooms ❖

15 to 20 large mushrooms (use caps and stems)
½ lb. Italian Sausage
1 tsp. Garlic chopped

Clean and de-stem mushrooms. Place caps upside down in glass baking dish.

Chop mushroom stems and garlic. Add to pork sausage.

Roll into 1-inch balls; place into the stem hole in mushrooms.

Bake at 350° for 25-30 minutes.

Serve as an appetizer or main dish

Serves 4-6.

❖ Basic Meatloaf ❖

2 lbs. ground round or ground sirloin

1 c. almond meal or 1 c. bread crumbs (p. 36)

½ c. water

1 egg

Salt and pepper to taste

In a medium bowl mix all ingredients.

Form meatloaf into a loaf pan; allow about ½ inch from pan sides so the juices do not spill over.

Bake at 350° for 1 hour.

This is moist and meaty and great cold on sandwiches!

Almond meal does not add or take away flavor from the meat.

For meatballs: add:

1 tsp. Italian seasoning

1 tsp. chopped garlic

❖ Meat and Bean Burritos ❖

6 flour crêpe/tortillas (p. 166)
1 can spicy refried beans (or favorite refried beans)
1 lb. cooked hamburger or ground turkey seasoned with salt & pepper
Chile powder to taste.
1 c. grated cheddar cheese
Green or red chile salsa (to taste)

Make basic crepe/tortilla recipe using an 8-inch frying pan.

Cool crêpe/tortilla on a wire rack. Re-heat just before filling.

Cook meat and seasonings thoroughly and drain.

Heat beans until bubbly.

Fill re-heated crêpe/tortilla, with beans, meat, cheese and salsa down the middle. Fold end and roll. Eat with a fork or in your hands.

Crêpe/tortillas freeze well.

Makes 6

❖ Chicken Florentine ❖

6 chicken breast halves
1 c. GF bread crumbs (page 36)
¼ c. parmesan cheese
1 tsp. Italian seasoning
1 batch Florentine sauce (page 18)

Mix all dry ingredients, roll chicken in 1 c. crumb mix to coat.

Place chicken pieces in an 11" by 13" glass baking dish.

Cover chicken with Florentine sauce. Sprinkle remaining bread crumbs on top.

Bake at 350° for 50-60 minutes and chicken is thoroughly cooked and sauce is bubbly.

Serve with rice or mashed potatoes.

Makes 6 servings.

Eye appealing, aromatic, easy.

❖ San Luis Obispo Chicken Chile Relleno ❖

6 chicken breasts
6 Anaheim chiles, fresh or canned
16 oz. jar chunky salsa
¼ lb. Monterey jack cheese sliced to fit inside the chiles

Roast chiles over hot coals until chile is blackened and blistered.

When cool, peel chiles and stuff with cheese.

Place chicken breasts on BBQ, cook over hot coals 10 minutes, 5 minutes each side. Remove meat from BBQ or broiler place in glass baking dish 11" by 13".

Place stuffed chiles on the chicken and pour salsa on top.

Bake 350° 35-45 minutes

You can also use a broiler for roasting chilis and to broil chicken.

❖ Green Chile Chicken ❖

- 1 whole frying chicken, skinned
- 1 medium onion chopped
- 1 can mild green chiles, chopped
- 1 tsp. salt
- 2 c. water or chicken stock
- 2 cloves garlic crushed
- 1 tsp. chile powder
- 2 Tbsp. olive oil

Sprinkle chicken with salt and chile powder.

Place in a large pot with hot olive oil and lightly brown the chicken.

Add all other ingredients and simmer 1½-2 hours until chicken falls off the bones. Remove bones and return chicken to re-heat in the sauce.

Serve with warm corn tortillas or rice and South of the Border Salad (p. 62).

❖ Pork Roast and Gravy ❖

1 3 lb. boneless pork loin roast
1 lg. onion quartered
Salt and pepper to taste

❖

Preheat oven to 325°. Place roast in baking dish with the onions. Salt and pepper to taste. Put into oven for about 1 hour 15 minutes, or until roast has reached 160°, on the meat thermometer. When proper temperature has been reached, remove roast from oven and drain juices to a small saucepan for gravy.

Gravy

Juices from roasted pork
1 c. water
2 Tbsp. potato starch for thickening
Salt and Pepper to taste

❖

Heat roast drippings over medium heat until it starts to bubble. Mix water and potato starch, add to saucepan, stirring constantly until gravy is thickened.

Potato starch thickens without overriding the flavors of any foods and it does not separate when chilled.

❖ Fish and Chips ❖

2 lbs. Fresh cod or thick flesh white fish
½ c. fine bread crumbs (p. 36)
¼ c. potato starch
½ tsp. paprika
¾ c. vegetable oil

Mix bread crumbs, potato starch and paprika in a flat dish.

Cut fish into finger size pieces, gorilla fingers, 1 ½ x 3 inches, rinse and pat dry.

Dip fish into bread crumb mixture, just to coat.

Heat oil to medium high in an 8-inch frying pan.

Fry about 5 pieces at a time. Makes about 10 pieces, serving 4 generous portions.

Chips (p.121)

❖ Eggplant Parmesan ❖

2 c. marinara Sauce (p. 21)
1 c. seasoned bread crumbs (p. 36)
1 egg
1 eggplant, cut into ¾″ thick, round slices
8 oz. mozzarella cheese, sliced
¼ c. parmesan cheese
Salt and pepper to taste

❖

In a pie plate beat egg with salt and pepper.

In another pie plate, pour seasoned bread crumbs and parmesan cheese. Mix.

Dip eggplant rounds into the egg, then into the seasoned bread-crumb mix. Turn over to cover both sides. Save excess bread crumbs for topping this casserole. Place in the bottom of a large 11x13 casserole.

Heat oven to 350°. Bake for 10 minutes, pour heated marinara sauce over the eggplant, return to oven continue baking 20 minutes. Top each eggplant slice with mozzarella cheese slices, sprinkle top with remaining bread crumbs. Put into oven; bake 5 minutes until the cheese is melted.

Serves 4-6 (main course) 6-8 (side-dish)

Truly delicious and fast.

❖ Beef Stroganoff ❖

½ c. potato starch
½ tsp. salt
1 lb. sirloin steak, cut into ½ inch strips
2 Tbsp. olive oil
2 c. sliced mushrooms
1 medium onion, chopped
1 clove garlic, minced
2 Tbsp. potato starch, dissolved in ½ c. water
1 Tbsp. tomato paste
1 c. water
1 c. sour cream
½ c. sherry

Dredge meat in potato starch, so meat is coated, salt lightly. Heat skillet or wok, add olive oil. Brown meat quickly, flipping to brown both sides. Add mushrooms, onion and garlic. Cook 3 to 4 minutes or until onions are tender. Remove from heat, pour meat into a small bowl, set aside.

Return pan to heat, pour in water, bring to boil, add tomato paste and potato starch water, stir until thickened. Return meat mixture into the gravy. Stir in sour cream and sherry, heat briefly. Serve over wide rice oriental noodles, fettuccini rice pasta, or homemade pasta.

This recipe is so fast that you should cook pasta at the same time.

❖ Shrimp and Fish Au Gratin ❖

3 1½ inch slices GF (day old or older) bread
2 Tbsp. olive oil
1 c. chopped celery
2 green onions, chopped
1 ½ tsp. dill weed, dried
1 clove garlic, minced
4 fillets of dense meat white fish, like cod or orange roughy
4 Tbsp. lemon juice
6 oz, shrimp, small, frozen, defrosted

Crumble bread; bake in 200° low oven, 30 minutes, to dry out.

Sauté celery, onions and garlic in olive oil. Add dill weed, pepper, water, shrimp and bread crumbs.

Place fish, skin side down in a buttered 9x12 baking dish. Sprinkle fish with lemon juice. Spoon bread mixture over fish.

Bake 350° for 30 minutes.

WARNING! DO NOT TRY THIS RECIPE WITH BREAD YOU BOUGHT AT THE HEALTH FOOD STORE—IF IT DIDN'T TASTE GOOD ON THE FIRST DAY, WHY RUIN ANOTHER DAY? Authors opinion.

Slow Cook

Turkey Mexicana

Pot Roast

High Sierra Pot Roast

Chinese Chicken

Pork Chile Verde

Slow Cook-Corned Beef

❖ Turkey Mexicana ❖

6 turkey thighs
1 16 oz. jar chile verde sauce
2 cloves garlic, crushed
1 c. water
3 Tbsp. corn starch for thickening (optional) + ½ c. water

❖

Place turkey at the bottom of the crock pot; add Verde sauce, water and garlic. When the turkey is cooked, thicken the broth by adding the cornstarch dissolved in water.

Garnish with lime and cilantro; serve with hot corn bread.

Cooking setting:	Low	6-8	hours
	Med	6-7	hours
	High	4-6	hours

Turkey is moist and tender, it can be used for a main dish or use in casseroles and enchiladas.

❖ Pot Roast ❖

1 3-4 lb. chuck roast
4 small onions, whole
1 tsp. paprika
6 medium potatoes
4-6 carrots, cut in half diagonally
5 c. water
salt and pepper to taste

❖

Put meat on the bottom of crock pot, add onions, water, paprika, and a little salt.

1 hour before serving, add potatoes and carrots. 10 minutes before serving, thicken with potato starch water.

Cooking setting:	Low	6-8	hours
	Med	6-7	hours
	High	4-6	hours

Potato starch water

3 Tbsp. potato starch dissolved in ¼ c. water

Potato starch water measurements vary based on liquid volume. If you want a thicker gravy, add more potato starch-water mix.

❖ High Sierra Pot Roast ❖

1 large pot roast
1 large can GF chile colorado
1 large onion, chopped
2 garlic cloves, whole

Cooking setting:	Low 6-8 hours
	Med 6-7 hours
	High 4-6 hours

This is a tasty tostada topper.

❖

Place pot roast on bottom of crock pot, add sauce, onion and garlic. Serve this on hot buttered rice linguini, and a salad.

❖ Chinese Chicken ❖

2 small frying chickens, cut up
1 onion, minced
6 c. water
2 Tbsp. GF soy sauce (**most soy sauces contain wheat)**
1 package Chinese vegetables, fresh if possible.
1 Tbsp. corn starch dissolved in ½ c. water.

❖

Place chicken and onions in the crock pot. Add water and soy sauce.

20 minutes before serving rinse vegetables, and add to pot. When vegetables are thoroughly heated, thicken with dissolved corn starch.

Cooking setting:	Low	6-8 hours
	Med	6-7 hours
	High	4-6 hours

Serve over a steaming bowl of rice. Add more soy sauce at the table, if desired.

❖ Pork Chile Verde ❖

1-2 lb. pork tri-tip, also called pork cushion

1 small can mild green chiles (chopped)

1 Tbsp. garlic, chopped

1 medium onion, chopped

1 small can tomatillos or 10 fresh tomatillos

1 tsp. salt

3 c. water

❖

Put everything in the crock pot.

Break meat apart by using 2 forks.

Cooking setting:	Low	6-8	hours
	Med	6-7	hours
	High	4-6	hours

Optional thickening: add 1 Tbsp. potato starch dissolved in ½ cup water just before serving.

Traditionally this is served in a bowl, alongside beans and tortillas.

❖ Slow Cook-Corned Beef Dinner ❖

1 2-5 lb. corned beef
6 c. water
1 lg. onion whole
2 celery ribs
Potatoes
Carrots

Place meat, onion and celery into the crock pot. Add 6 cups water (or enough water to cover the meat). Turn crock pot to low setting. Cook 6-8 hours.

Prepare potatoes and carrots, by washing or peeling. Add 1 hour before serving.

Bridgeford Farms identifies their corned beef as Gluten Free.

Cakes, Cookies & other Sweets

Morro Rock Bundt Cake

Applesauce Bundt Cake

Carrot Cake

Mock Graham Cracker Crust

Flan (Carmel Custard)

Hazelnut Cookies (Filbertines)

3 Ingredient Almond Cookie

Piano Keys

Flour-Free Peanut Butter Chocolate Chip Cookies

Brownies

Raspberry Bars

Coconut Macaroons

Diamond Lil's Pecan Bar

Criss Cross Peanut Butter Cookies

❖ Morro Rock Bundt Cake ❖

2 c. GF bread flour mix (p. 13)
2 tsp. xanthan gum
¼ c. powdered baking chocolate
6 eggs
2 c. sugar
1 ½ c. butter, softened
1 tsp. baking powder

Preheat oven to 350°

Cream butter and sugar together in a large mixing bowl, add 1 egg at a time mixing on high speed with electric mixer until light and fluffy.

Sift all dry ingredients together. Add to butter, sugar and eggs.

By hand, stir in dry ingredients until well blended. Pour batter into a non-stick bundt pan. Bake 60-65 minutes. Check for doneness with toothpick.

Remove from oven, cool 2 minutes, remove from pan and cool on a wire rack for 2 hours. Frost if desired.

This cake never fails to amaze me!

❖ Applesauce Bundt Cake ❖

2 c. GF bread flour mix (p. 13)
2 tsp. xanthan gum
1 egg
1 c. sugar
1 ½ c. chunky applesauce
3/4 c. butter, softened
1 tsp. baking powder
½ tsp. vanilla powder of 1 tsp. GF vanilla
1 tsp. cinnamon
½ tsp. cloves
½ tsp. nutmeg
1 c. raisins (optional)

Cream butter and sugar together in a large mixing bowl, add egg. Mix on high speed with electric mixer until light and fluffy.

Sift all dry ingredients together. Add to butter, sugar and eggs.

By hand, stir in dry ingredients until well blended. Pour batter into a non-stick bundt pan. Bake 60-65 minutes. Or use 6 mini bundt cakes. Bake 30 minutes. Check for doneness with toothpick.

Remove from oven, cool 2 minutes, remove from pan and cool on a wire rack for 2 hours.

Dust with powdered sugar.

❖ *Carrot Cake* ❖

Good

8" pan

still too sweet (used ¾ c)

½ c ¾ c. vegetable oil

¾ c 1 c. sugar

2 eggs

1 c. GF bread flour mix (p. 13)

1 tsp. xanthan gum *½ tsp gum g*

1 tsp. baking powder

1 c. finely grated carrots

Pinch of salt

½ tsp. cinnamon

½ tsp. cloves

¼ tsp. nutmeg

½ c. walnuts (optional) *+ raisins that sank to bottom of pan*

Icing

1 lb. powdered sugar

1 tsp. vanilla GF

1 8 oz. pack cream cheese, softened

Preheat oven to 350°.

Combine oil and sugar in a large mixing bowl, beat on high. Add eggs, beat until light and airy.

Sift dry ingredients together, gradually add to sugar, oil, and egg mix.

Fold in carrots.

Pour into a 9-inch round non-stick pan.

Bake 50-60 minutes. Check for doneness.

Cool on wire rack for 1 hour and ice.

❖

Icing: mix all icing ingredients in a small bowl, until blended. Ice sides of cake then the top. Sprinkle with chopped nuts. (optional)

❖ Mock Graham Cracker Crust ❖

1 c. almond meal
1 c. buckwheat, medium grind
4 Tbsp. butter, softened
½ c. sugar
½ tsp. vanilla

Put all ingredients into a small bowl. Mix with a fork until all of the dry ingredients are covered with butter.

Pour into an 8 or 9 inch pie pan. Firmly press crumbs against the edges and the bottom of the pan. Bake at 400° for 10 minutes.

Remove from oven and cool. Use just as a graham cracker crust.

❖ Flan (Carmel Custard) ❖

1/3 c. sugar
6 eggs
6 Tbsp. sugar
2 c. milk
1 tsp. GF vanilla

❖

In a small frying pan, over medium heat melt 1/3 cup sugar, shake pan instead of stirring. Once melted, sugar caramelizes quickly. When it caramelizes, pour into 8-inch pie pan. Do not worry if it gets too dry. It will soften while baking.

Preheat oven to 350°

Beat together eggs, 6 Tbsp. sugar, milk and vanilla.

Set the carmel lined pan in hot bath (see below). Pour in egg mixture. Bake about 25 minutes. Flan is done when top splits in center. Split is about ½ inch deep.

To make hot bath: *Use a pan larger than the flan pan, fill about ½ inch with hot water.*

❖ Hazelnut Cookies (Filbertines) ❖

½ c. butter, softened
½ c. sugar
1 egg
1 1/3 c. GF bread flour mix (p. 13)
1 tsp. xanthan gum
½ tsp. baking powder
1/8 tsp. ground cardamom
½ c. ground hazelnuts (**this is becoming very easy to find in specialty food stores**).

In a small mixing bowl, cream butter and sugar. Beat in egg.

Combine the flour, baking powder, xanthan gum and cardamom. Add to creamed mixture. Cover and refrigerate for 1 hour.

Shape into 1-in. balls; roll in ground nuts. Place 2 inches apart on prepared baking sheets.

Bake 350° for 15-18 mins. or lightly browned. Cool on wire racks.

Yields 3 dozen.

❖ 3 Ingredient Almond Cookie ❖

3 c. ground almonds (available in most specialty stores)
1 ½ c. sugar
3 eggs

Preheat oven to 350°.

Mix all ingredients together. Spoon onto prepared cookie sheets with a medium size spoon.

Bake 20 minutes, until edges are brown.

Yields 3 dozen.

❖ Piano Keys ❖

12 Green Pea Flavor Rice Crackers
1 4 oz. semi-sweet GF chocolate baking bar

❖

Melt chocolate in a double boiler or microwave. Dip rice crackers, lengthwise into chocolate, about ½ inch. Cool on wax paper.

The chocolate is easy to find in the baking section of most supermarkets.

The cookies (Green Pea Flavor Rice Crackers) are found in Oriental markets in the cracker section. The label says "soy" however my research with the manufacturer, Sunny Maid Corp., says, "no soy."

This chocolate and these cookies are good enough on their own, but jazzy as piano keys.

❖ Flour-Free Peanut Butter Chocolate Chip Cookies ❖

1 c. peanut butter, chunky or creamy (read the label)
1 c. brown sugar, tightly packed
1 lg. egg, slightly beaten
1 c. semi sweet chocolate chips (read the label)

Heat oven to 350°.
In a medium size bowl, mix eggs, sugar and peanut butter. Stir in chocolate chips. Spoon onto un-greased cookie sheets spacing cookies about 2 inches apart. Bake 10 minutes. Cookies will be soft and golden.
Remove from oven, cool on cookie sheet 5 minutes, and transfer to wire rack to continue cooling.
Makes 3 dozen.

WARNING! Chocolate chips remain hot for a long period of time.
KEEP KIDS OUT.

❖ Brownies ❖

2/3 c. GF bread flour mix (p. 13)
½ tsp. xanthan gum
¾ c. sugar
¼ tsp. vanilla powder or 1 tsp. GF vanilla
½ c. butter, softened
¾ c. GF cocoa mix (available in most markets)
¼ tsp. salt
2 eggs

Preheat oven to 350°.

In a large mixing bowl cream sugar and butter with electric mixer, add eggs. Beat until creamy.

Sift all dry ingredients and fold into the egg mixture. Stir until just moistened.

Spread into a buttered 8 or 9 inch square-baking pan.

Bake 20-30 minutes. Brownie top should be shiny and toothpick dry when testing for doneness.

The brownies, pictured in this book, were baked in a 9-inch square pan. These brownies taste as good as they look.

❖ Raspberry Bars ❖

1 c. buckwheat cereal (medium grind)
1 c. almond meal
½ c. brown sugar
½ c. butter, softened
1 c. raspberry preserves (check label)

Preheat oven 350°.

In a medium size bowl, mix buckwheat, almond meal, brown sugar and butter, until thoroughly mixed.

Pat mixture into a 9 inch square pan. Bake 25 minutes.

Remove pan from oven, spoon preserves over the top of the crust, return to oven for 15 minutes.

Crust should be medium brown and slightly crunchy.

Cool 2 hours before cutting.

Makes 9-3 inch squares.

Pack these in the lunch box!

❖ Coconut Macaroons ❖

1 lb. coconut, flaked (read label)
½ c. sweetened condensed milk
1 tsp. vanilla or ¼ tsp. vanilla powder

In a large bowl, mix coconut, milk and vanilla. Chill for 30 minutes or overnight.

Preheat oven to 350°.

Line cookie sheets with parchment cooking paper, *or don't make these cookies!*

Drop by spoonful onto lined cookie sheet.

Bake 12-15 minutes. Macaroon tops should have some golden flakes and bottom sticky. When macaroons are cooled, remove from paper.

Makes 3 dozen.

Tip: Remove cookie sheet from oven, transfer the macaroons and parchment paper directly to a wire rack for cooling.

❖ Diamond Lil's Pecan Bar ❖

1/3 c. butter, 4 Tbsp. butter
1 egg
¼ c. sugar
1 c. bread flour mix (p. 13)
½ c. ground almond flour
1 tsp. xanthan gum
1/3 c. brown sugar, firmly packed
3 Tbsp. sugar
1/3 tsp. honey
2 Tbsp. heavy cream
1 c. pecans, coarsely chopped

Preheat oven 375°.

Mix bread flour mix, almond flour and xanthan gum.

Beat 1/3 c. butter in a small bowl, add sugar. Beat with electric mixer until light and fluffy. Beat in egg. Stir in flour, mixing well, until a soft dough forms. Spread evenly in a 9-inch square pan.

Bake for 12 minutes, until the dough just starts to set, but is not fully cooked. Remove to wire rack. Lower oven temperature to 350°.

(Continued next page)

Diamond Lil's Pecan Bars Continued

Meanwhile, melt remaining butter in a medium sized saucepan. Add brown sugar, 3 Tbsp. sugar and honey. Bring to boiling and continue boiling 2 ½ minutes. Mixture will be thick and caramel colored. Carefully add cream and bring back to boiling. Remove from heat, stir in pecans.

Spread mixture evenly over cookie dough. Return to oven, bake 25 minutes or until pecan mixture is bubbly and begins to set.

Remove to wire rack, cool completely, pecan topping will become firm upon cooling. Cut 8 lengthwise strips and 9 diagonal strips to make the diamond shape.

Makes 4 dozen

Good & easy!

❖ Criss Cross Peanut Butter Cookies ❖

2 1/4 c. GF bread flour mix (p. 13)
~~2~~ 1 tsp. xanthan gum
1 c. creamy peanut butter
2/3 c. brown sugar, firmly packed
½ c. sugar
½ c. butter
2 eggs
1 ½ tsp. baking powder
1 tsp vanilla
1/2 tsp salt

Preheat oven to 350°.

In a large bowl, mix all ingredients with mixer on medium speed. Beat well.

Shape into 1 ½ balls, place 3 inches apart on cookie sheets.

Using a fork, press deeply across cookie, repeat in opposite direction, creating a cross pattern.

Bake 12 minutes for soft, 15 minutes for chewy.

Makes about 3 dozen.

Sweet Things

Basic Crêpes

Crêpes Fillings

Chocolate Mocha Mousse

Orange Cream Filling

Crêpes Orange Juice Syrup

English Toffee

Strawberry Ice

❖ Crêpes ❖

1 c. milk
¾ c. GF bread flour mix (p. 13)
2 large eggs
½ tsp. xanthan gum
Pinch of salt

❖

In blender container, combine all ingredients and process until smooth; let stand for 15-20 minutes. This batter can be whisked in a mixing bowl.

Heat an 8-inch non-stick skillet, medium (to test: sprinkle skillet with drop of water, if water sizzles skillet is hot enough).

Pour ¼ cup of batter into skillet and quickly swirl batter so that it covers entire bottom of pan.

Cook over medium high heat until edges and underside are dry.

Using a pancake turner, carefully turn crêpe over, cook other side briefly just to dry, about 30 seconds.

Slide crêpe onto a wire rack and let cool. Repeat procedure using remaining batter.

Makes 8

Fillings for crêpes can be very sweet, that's why these recipes are in the sweets section!

❖ Crêpes Fillings ❖

Chocolate Mocha Mouse

1 c. ricotta cheese
2 Tbsp. sugar
1 tsp. freeze dried coffee
2 Tbsp. GF sweet ground chocolate

In a small bowl combine all of the ingredients, stir, set aside for 5 minutes, stir again, repeat if coffee has not completely dissolved. Fills two 8-inch crêpes. Dust chocolate mocha mouse crêpes with more sweet ground chocolate.

Orange Cream Filling

1 ½ c. ricotta cheese
1 tsp. sugar
1 tsp. orange zest

In a small bowl, combine cheese, sugar and zest. Fills three 8-inch crêpes. (photo p. 98).

❖ Crêpes Syrup ❖

Orange Juice Syrup

1 orange + enough juice to make ½ c. orange juice.

1 Tbsp. sugar

1 tsp. orange zest

1/8 tsp. xanthan gum

Juice an orange. Measure the orange juice, if not one half cup, add more orange juice.

Put the juice into a small saucepan. Scrape some of the meat from the orange into the pan; add sugar and orange zest. Bring to a quick boil and turn off heat. Stir in xanthan gum to thicken syrup.

Zest is the bright orange part of the peeling that has been freshly grated. Just the outer edge of the orange!

❖ English Toffee ❖

½ lb. butter
¼ c. boiling water
1 c. sugar
1 c. salted toasted almonds or pecans
½ tsp. baking soda
4 oz. semi sweet chocolate baking bar
¼ c. finely chopped toasted almonds or pecans

❖

Melt butter in heavy 2 qt. Saucepan: let it bubble up. Remove from heat; add water. Return to heat; bring to a boil and stir in sugar. Cook over medium heat, stirring to 280° (soft crack stage). Add salted nuts. Continue cooking, stirring to 300° (hard crack stage). Remove from heat; stir in soda.

Pour mixture into a large buttered cookie sheet. Cool. When hard, remove from pan in one piece.

Melt chocolate over hot (not boiling water) double boiler technique. Spread half of the chocolate on one side of cooled candy. Sprinkle with half of the finely chopped nuts. Refrigerate until chocolate is set. Coat other side with chocolate and nuts.

Yield: 1-¼ pounds, 3-4 dozen pieces.

Note: Too slow cooking or damp weather will cause butter to separate out; if this occurs, candy is fine, just pour off butter while still warm. For best results, do not make English toffee on rainy or humid days.

This treat has been given to family and friends for over 30 years but never the recipe.

❖ Strawberry Ice ❖

5 c. fresh strawberries
2/3 c. sugar
2/3 c. water
¼ c. lemon juice

Place strawberries in blender or food processor; cover and process until smooth.

In a saucepan, heat sugar and water until sugar is dissolved, pour into blender. Add lemon juice, cover and process until combined.

Pour into a shallow plastic freezer container, 7x5 works great, and cover. Freeze.

Use later in smothies or as a fresh strawberry syrup.

Beverages

Strawberry Banana Smoothie

Peaches & Cream Smoothie

Mocha Java Smoothie

Mock Kahlua

Mock Grand Marnier

Iced Tea

Mimosas

❖ Strawberry Banana Smoothie ❖

1 c. strawberries
1 banana, freckled but not too ripe
1 c. plain yogurt
1 c. ice cubes

Put all ingredients into a blender, set chop cycle ½ minute, frappe 1 minute. Yields 2 glasses.

❖ Peaches & Cream Smoothie ❖

1 large peach, peeled and pit removed
½ c. ricotta cheese or ½ c. yogurt
½ c. ice cubes

Put all ingredients into a blender, set chop cycle ½ minute, frappe 1 minute. Yields 1 glass.

❖ Mocha Java Smoothie ❖

1 c. plain yogurt (or GF vanilla ice cream)
1 Tbsp. instant coffee
1 Tbsp. sweet ground chocolate
½ c. ice cubes

Put all ingredients into a blender, set chop cycle ½ minute, frappe 1 minute. Yields 1 glass.

❖ Mock Kahlua ❖

3 c. water
4 c. sugar
4 oz. instant, freeze dried coffee
1 vanilla bean
1 7.5 liter bottle GF vodka **(most vodka is made from grain, not potato)**

Bring sugar and water to a boil until sugar is dissolved. Take off stove. Add coffee. Stir until dissolved. Cool.

Add vodka and stir. Pour all of the liquid into a larger bottle. Slice vanilla bean in half, lengthwise. Insert the vanilla bean. Put the top on the bottle and age kahlua for 3 months.

❖ Mimosas ❖

Champagne Orange juice Ice cubes	Per glass: 4-5 ice cubes add 2 oz. orange juice, 2 oz. champagne (in that order).

❖ Iced Tea ❖

4 tea bags 2 c. boiling water 4 c. ice cubes 4 c. water	Steep tea in boiling water for 3 minutes. In a large pitcher add ice and water. When tea is finished steeping, remove bags and pour steeped tea into the pitcher, stir and serve in tall glasses with a lemon wedge.

Dips, Spreads & Snacks

San Francisco French Garlic Spread

Gilroy Garlic Growers Reply

Cheese Crackers with Flax Seeds

Buckwheat Thins

Party Wings

Crab Dip

Cottage Cheese and Dill Dip

Dill Pickles

❖ San Francisco French Garlic Spread ❖

1 cube butter, softened
1 tsp. garlic, minced
¼ c. grated parmesan cheese
1 loaf french bread (p. 43)

Mix butter and garlic in a small bowl. Cut bread in half lengthwise and spread both halves with garlic butter. Sprinkle with parmesan cheese. Toast under broiler until golden. Slice and serve.

❖ Gilroy Garlic Growers Reply ❖

1 cube butter, softened
Gilroy garlic, minced
¼ c. grated parmesan cheese
1 loaf french bread (p. 43)

Mix butter and ADD MORE GILROY GARLIC in a small bowl.

Cut bread in half lengthwise and spread both halves with garlic butter. Sprinkle with parmesan cheese. Toast under broiler until golden. Slice and serve. *Thank You Gilroy.*

❖ Cheese Crackers with Flax Seeds ❖

1 c. bread flour mix (p. 13)
1 c. grated parmesan cheese
5 Tbsp. butter
1 lg. egg
1/8 tsp. ground pepper
2 Tbsp. Flax seeds

❖

Preheat oven 350°.

In food processor whirl butter, cheese, flour and pepper, until fine crumbs form. Add egg and flax seeds, whirl until dough holds together, pat into a ball. Divide dough in half; pat ½ of the dough into a rectangle and place between 1 piece of wax paper and 1 sheet of cooking parchment. Roll until dough is about 1/6 inch thick. Piece should be about 15x10 inches.

Lift away wax paper, trim edges of dough so sides are straight. Score dough with a knife or pizza cutter into about 1" squares.

Bake about 15 minutes, until crackers are light brown and bubble up. Remove crackers and parchment to cool on a wire rack. After cooling, break crackers apart at the score line.

While first batch is baking, prepare second batch. Store in an airtight container in the pantry.

Makes a ton of little crackers.

If your kids love little cheese fish crackers they will love these too.

❖ Buckwheat Thins ❖

1 c. GF bread flour mix (p. 13)
½ c. buckwheat, medium grind
½ c. parmesan cheese
5 Tbsp. butter
1 large egg

❖

In a food processor, blend on low the first 4 ingredients. When pea size crumbs form, add egg.

Continue blending until dough forms. Divide dough in half.

Use 1 sheet parchment paper and 1 sheet wax paper. Form the dough into a square on top of the parchment, cover with wax paper. Roll the dough with a rolling pin until the dough is about 1/6 inch thick.

Lift wax paper away and cut 1 ½ squares into the dough. Use a pizza cutter or a knife.

Bake 15 minutes. Crackers will be golden brown. Remove crackers and parchment to a wire rack to cool.

While first batch is baking prepare the second batch.

Store in an airtight container.

Makes about 70 1-½ inch square crackers.

These sturdy little crackers travel well. Another lunchbox treat!

❖ Party Wings ❖

12 chicken wings, fresh or frozen, defrosted
1 c. potato starch
1 Tbsp. chile powder
1 tsp. salt

Wash and pat dry, chicken wings.

Mix potato starch, chile powder and salt in a large plastic bag. Add 2 or 3 wings to the bag and shake until chicken is coated. Place coated chicken on a lined cookie sheet. Repeat until all wings are coated.

Bake, 375° for 20 minutes, turn wings, and return to oven. Continue cooking until done. About 20 minutes. Remove from oven. Cut each wing in two.

Dip: Mix in a small bowl, ¼ c. sour cream, ½ tsp. hot sauce, or salsa, 1 tsp. chile powder.

Makes 24 pieces.

❖ Crab Dip ❖

1 c. GF mayonnaise
½ c. sour cream
1 Tbsp. sherry
1 tsp. lemon juice
1 6/12 oz. can crabmeat, drained
Salt and pepper to taste

Combine all ingredients, chill 2 hours or more, serve.

There is a national brand of crabmeat without MSG, if you are sensitive to gluten you may be sensitive to MSG.

❖ Cottage Cheese and Dill Dip ❖

1 pint cottage cheese (read label for modified food starch)
1 tsp. dill weed, dried

Combine both ingredients. Serve with huge carrot coins or chips.

❖ Dill Pickles ❖

2 quarts water
2 quarts cider vinegar
1 c. plain salt (UN-iodized)
Fresh dill weed
3-4 garlic cloves, per quart jar (optional)

Pickling cucumbers*
*Number per jar is based on cucumber size.

Makes about 7 quarts

Prepare and pack jars with dill weed sprigs, garlic, and cucumbers.

In a large pot, bring water, vinegar and salt to rolling boil. Ladle brining mixture to each jar filling to the rim. Seal the jar.

Ready in 6 weeks.

To add variety to these pickles, add prepared pickling spices. Most food stores carry this packet in the spice section.

Have Questions about Products?

You have more questions now than you can imagine. You have the right to ask restaurants, pharmacies, and manufacturers of food products about the contents of anything that you will ingest.

Don't feel that you are imposing on their exclusive rights to produce a product that they won't guarantee is not going to make you ill.

Go shopping with a note pad:

- Write the name of the company
- Phone number, most will have a toll free number on the packaging
- Name of the product
- Possible problem ingredients, such as Modified Food Starch

Call the company: Ask for a dietician, RD, or chemist on staff. Tell them that you are calling to identify the food that modifies their product, the food base could be wheat and that is what you are avoiding. The food base could also be corn, and that is usually not a problem. Food companies are especially helpful because they do not want you to get sick.

For example, I called a "major chocolate factory" to make certain that all of the chocolate that I use is GF. The representatives told me that the chocolate that is in my diet is GF, but the white chocolates that they manufacture are not.

I know this is time consuming, but your health is much too important not to take that time.

Choose a Pharmacy that understands your condition. Tell them that if they don't have the time to research a product, you will do it. Ask them for the toll free number.
Pharmaceutical companies are somewhat more hesitant to give out trade, or patented information. But when they know that you are avoiding gluten, they will generally say that it is GF or not.

Restaurants are becoming aware that there are food allergies that are deadly serious. They are more willing to answer questions about their kitchens and their products but it is up to you to ask!

Even cruise ships are making GF dieting safe and easy. Life is getting better all the time.

Glossary of Terms

al dente: An Italian term that means "to the teeth", in cooking it means the food is biting tender.

Bake: To cook uncovered in an oven.

Baking Powder: A leavening agent, used to make foods rise. Doubling acting baking powder (used i recipes in this book) produces gas bubbles twice, once during mixing and second during baking.

Baking Soda: A leavening agent essential in baking powder. Used alone in mixtures containing acid such as tomatoes – it acts as a neutralizer. Baking soda reacts as soon as it comes in contact with liquid

Blend: To mix thoroughly two or more ingredients, or to be prepared in a blender until pureed.

Boil: 1. To cook water to 212° at sea level. 2. To cook food over high heat in liquid bubbles rise to th surface and break.

Bread: To coat with bread crumbs, cracker crumbs or cornmeal.

Buckwheat: A triangular shape, not grain, used to make cereal (kasha) or ground for flour.

Caramelize: To stir or shake sugar in a skillet over low-to-medium heat until it melts and turns a golden brown

Chill: To refrigerate food or let it stand in ice, or iced water until cold.

Chop: To cut food into small pieces with a knife, blender or food processor.

Coat: To sprinkle food with, or dip into flour until covered.

Coins: To cut a vegetable horizontally about 1/4 in. shaping a coin.

Cool: To refrigerate food, or let stand at room temperature, until no longer warm.

Cream: 1. The fat portion of milk. 2. To make smooth and creamy by beating with a spoon or mixer.

Crêpe: A thin delicate pancake.

Crouton: A small cube of toasted bread used to garnish soups and salads.

Cube: 1. To cut food into small cubes about ½ inch. 2. ¼ lb. cube of butter packaged for table use.

Dice: To cut food into very small pieces about ¼ inch.

Dijon mustard: prepared mustard (originally made in Dijon France) mild to highly seasoned.

Dollops: Large spoonful of batter or whipped cream. Usually for decoration.

Dredge: To cover or coat food, as with flour, cornmeal, etc.

Fillet: A piece of boneless, meat, fish or poultry.

Flour: *Avoid wheat!* 1. For the purpose of this book, flour will mean flours and starches derived from beans, rice, corn, potato and tapioca. 2. To coat lightly with flour.

Fold in: To combine delicate ingredients like whipped cream or egg whites using a gentle circular motio to mix into a denser mixture, to create volume and lightness.

Freeze-dried: Term applied to food that has been dried by rapid freezing, removing most of its wate content.

Garnish: To add a decorative touch to food.

Grate: To rub food on a grater to produce fine, medium or coarse particles.

Grind: To reduce to particles in food grinder, blender or food processor.

Invert: To turn over.

Julienne: To cut a vegetable in long strips, also called shoestring cut.

Lukewarm: At a temperature of about 95°.

Milk: Pasteurized cows milk, available fresh, canned and dried.

Mince: To cut into very fine pieces using knife, food grinder or blender.

Mocha: Flavoring for coffee.

Pasta: Spaghetti types of products, made of rice, corn and beans. For the sake of this book; rice past products are from Canada and U.S.A. Noodles from Asia.

Peel: To remove outer coverings of foods by trimming with a knife, vegetable peeler or pulling by hand.

Pit: To remove pit from the whole fruit.

Puree: A thick mixture made from a pureed vegetable base, usually tomatoes.

Score: 1. To cut shallow slits in surface of food to increase tenderness. 2. To cut to mark areas that are to be broken away to create a shape.

Simmer: To cook food over low heat in a liquid just below the boiling point in which bubbles form slowly and collapse just below the surface.

Steam: To cook food on a rack or colander in a covered pan over steaming hot water.

Sugar: Cane or beet sugars used in several forms: Granulated unless otherwise specified in this book is the table sugar used in cooking. Confectioners, or powdered sugar, used for frosting or dusting outsides of cakes, cookies and doughnuts. Brown sugars can be white sugar colored by molasses. The recipes in this book use naturally brown sugar.

Tortilla: Very thin, Mexican bread made of cornmeal or flour. The crêpe recipe in this book can be used in lieu of a commercial flour tortilla.

Toss: To mix foods lightly with a lifting motion, using two forks or spoons.

Tostada: Corn tortilla, fried until crisp, served flat. Topped with refried beans and other fresh toppings.

Vinegar: An acid liquid used for flavorings and preserving. Many varieties including cider, made from apples, white, made from grain alcohol and red and white wine vinegars.

Whip: To beat rapidly with mixer, wire whisk or hand beater.

Wok: Chinese cooking utensil with rounded bottom used as a skillet.

Xanthan gum: The white powder that binds GF flours together.

Yeast: Microorganisms that produce a chemical reaction that cause baked goods to rise. Recipes in this book call for rapid rise active dry yeast.

Zest: The outer most colorful edge of citrus fruits, peeled or scraped to add flavor and color to baked breads, etc.

Index

ebelskiver
Basic recipe, 56
pples
pple muffins, 24,
pple cobbler crisp, 31
pple mini bundt cake photo, 998
pple mini bundt cake recipe, 151
pplesauce Bundt Cake, 151
aguettes, 42
asic mix recipe, 13
asic recipe, 42
Photos 104,112
asic Mixes
read dough mix,13
sandwich bun mix, 13
pizza dough mix, 13
asic GF Kitchen
asic kitchen, 12
eef
Meat and bean burritos, 132
Meatloaf, 131
Stuffed peppers, 127
Swiss steak bake, 126
Stroganoff, 139
Slow cook corned beef, 147
Pastrami on *Rye, 82
Pot roast, 143
High Sierra pot roast, 144

Beverages
Strawberry smoothie, 172
Peaches & Cream smoothie, 172
Mocha java smoothie, 173
Mock Kahula, 173
Mimosas, 174
Iced Tea, 174
Biscuits
Basic biscuits, 34
Mustard sesame, 35
Cranberry orange sticky buns, 53
Breads, quick
Apple muffin, 24
Blueberry muffins, 25
Lemon poppy seed muffins, 26
Waffles, 28
Doughnuts, 29
Banana bread, 32
Corn bread and muffins, 33
Biscuits, 34
Breads, yeast
Crowning white bread, 38
Dark *Rye, 39
Golden almond, 40
Light *Rye, 41
Hamburger buns, 42
Sandwich rolls, 42
Baguette/Submarine rolls, 42
French Bread, 43
Pizza dough, 44

Breakfast
Aebelskiver, 56
Apple cobbler crisp, 31
Banana bread, 32
Biscuits, 34
Bread Pudding, 51
Buckwheat cereal, 47
Cranberry orange sticky buns, 53
Crepes, 166
Doughnuts, 30
Eggs Ole, 49
Ham and cheese casserole, 54
Huevos Rancheros, 50
Muffins, 24, 25, 26, 33
Pancakes, 27, 29
Seafood Omelet, 55
Waffles, 28
Broccoli, see vegetables
Buckwheat (Kasha)
Buckwheat cereal, 47
Buckwheat thins, 178
Mock graham cracker crust, 153
Raspberry Bars, 160
Cakes
Applesauce bundt, 151
Carrot cake, 152
Morro Rock Bundt Cake, 150

Casseroles
- Chicken Florentine, 133
- Chile Relleno Cassserole, 52
- Eggplant Parmesan, 138
- Eggs Ole, 49
- Ham and Cheese Casserole, 54
- Shrimp and Fish Au Gratin, 140

Chicken
- Cantaloupe and Curried Chicken Salad, 65
- Chicken Florentine, 133
- Chinese Chicken Slow Cook, 145
- Chinese Chicken Salad, 66
- Cream of Chicken Soup, 71
- Curried Chicken Salad, 65
- Green Chile Chicken, 135
- Grilled Chicken Caesar Salad, 63
- Party Wings, 180
- San Luis Obispo Chicken Chile Relleno, 134

Chocolate
- Brownies, 159
- Chocolate Crepe Filling, 167
- English Toffee, 169
- Flour-free peanut butter, chocolate chip cookies, 158
- Mocha Java Smoothie, 173
- Morro Rock Bundt Cake, 150
- Piano Keys, 157

Color Photo Pages 97-112

Cookies
- Coconut macaroons, 161
- Criss cross peanut butter, 164
- Flour free peanut butter, chocolate chip, 158
- Hazelnut Cookies, Filbertines, 155
- Piano Keys, 157
- 3 Ingredient Almond Cookies, 156

Crab, see fish and seafood

Crackers, see snacks

Cranberries, see fruits

Crêpes
- Basic crêpes, 166
- Grilled Chicken Caesar Salad, 63
- Fillings, 166
- Meat and bean burritos, 132

Desserts, see Sweets, Cakes, Cookies

Dips, see snacks

Eggs
- Amelia's Deviled Eggs, 46
- Eggs Ole, 49
- Egg Salad, 80
- Ham and Cheese Casserole, 54
- Huevos Rancheros, 50
- Seafood Omelet, 55
- Spaghetti All'uova, 95

Entrees, see Main Dishes

Fish and Seafood
- Baked Salmon in Dill Sauce, 129
- Crab Dip, 180
- Crab & Shrimp Sea Shell Pasta Salad, 96
- Salmon Salad, 81
- Seafood Omelet, 55
- Shrimp and Fish Au Gratin, 140
- Tuna Salad, 79

Fruits
- Apple muffins, 24
- Apple cobbler crisp, 31
- Apple mini bundt cake photo, 98
- Apple mini bundt cake recipe, 151
- Banana Bread, 32
- Blueberry Muffins, 25
- Applesauce Bundt Cake, 151
- Cantaloupe and Curried Chicken Salad, 65
- Cranberry orange sticky buns, 53
- Crepes, 166
- Lemon Poppy Seed Muffins, 26
- Mimosas, 174
- Pasta Spirals with Raspberr Dressing and Fruit, 64
- Peaches & Cream smoothie, 172
- Strawberry smoothie, 172

Jams, Jellies and Preserves, 83

Lasagna, see Pasta

Macaroni, see Pasta

Main Dishes
- Baked Salmon in Dill Sauce, 129
- Crab and Shrimp Seashell Past Salad, 96
- Italian Sausage Stuffed Mushrooms, 13

eat and bean burritos, 132
Meatloaf, 131
Stuffed peppers, 127
Swiss steak bake, 126
Stroganoff, 139
Slow cook corned beef, 147
Pot roast, 143
High Sierra pot roast, 144
Spaghetti All'uova, 95
easures and Measurements, 22
eats, see individual headings
exican dishes
Huevos Rancheros, 50
Meat and Bean Burritos, 132
San Luis Obispo Chicken Chile Relleno, 134
South of the Border Salad, 62
Turkey Mexicana, 142
uffins
Apple muffin, 24
Blueberry muffins, 25
Lemon poppy seed muffins, 26
Corn bread and muffins, 33
nions, see vegetables
ranges, see fruits
asta
Introduction to Pastas, 86-88
Chinese Chicken Salad, 66
Crab and Shrimp Sea Shell Pasta Salad, 96
Lasagna, 92
Lemon Linguini, 94
Pasta Pizza Salad, 90
Pasta Spirals with Raspberry Dressing and Fruit, 64
Pasta y Frigoli, Hearty Lentil Soup, 73
Spaghetti All'uova, 95
Spaghetti and Meatballs, 93
Spinach Stuffed Lasagna Rolls, 91
3 Cheese Macaroni Bake
Vegetable Pasta Salad, 68
Peanut Butter
Criss Cross Peanut Butter Cookies, 164
No Flour Peanut Butter and Chocolate Chip Cookies, 158
Peanut Butter and Jelly Sandwich, 83
Peppers, see vegetables
Pickles, see snacks
Pizza
Step by step directions in photo section, 110
Basic mix, 13
Recipe, 44
Potatoes and Rice
Creamy Potatoes & Broccoli Bake, 117
Dilled Potato Salad, 120
Garlic Mashed Potatoes, 119
Potato Wedges, oven fries, 121
Rissoto, 114
San Diego Mashed Potatoes, 116
Scalloped Potatoes, 122
Sour Cream and Onion Bake, 123
Twice Baked Potato with Zip, 115
Two Timing Rice and Potatoes, 118
Pork
Deviled Pork Chops, 128
Ham & Cheese Submarine Sandwich, 78
Italian Sausage Stuffed Mushrooms, 130
Pork Chile Verde, 146
Pork Roast with Gravy, 136
Poultry
Cantaloupe and Curried Chicken Salad, 65
Chicken Florentine, 133
Chinese Chicken Slow Cook, 145
Chinese Chicken Salad, 66
Cream of Chicken Soup, 71
Curried Chicken Salad, 65
Green Chile Chicken, 135
Grilled Chicken Caesar Salad, 63
Meat and Bean Burritos, 132
Party Wings, 180
San Luis Obispo Chicken Chile Relleno, 134
Turkey Mexicana, 142

Quick Breads, see Breads

Rice, see Potatoes and Rice

Salads and dressings
Coleslaw, 61
Crab and Shrimp Sea Shell Pasta Salad, 96
Croutons, 67
Egg Salad, 80
Cantaloupe and Curried Chicken Salad, 65
Chinese Chicken Salad, 66
Grilled Chicken Caesar Salad, 63
Pasta Pizza Salad, 90
Pasta Spirals with Raspberry Dressing and Fruit, 64
Salmon Salad, 81
South of the Border, 62
Spinach Salad, 59
Tuna Salad, 79
Vegetable Pasta Salad, 68
Sandwiches
Egg Salad, 80
Ham and Cheese Sub, 78
Pastrami on *Rye, 82
Peanut Butter and Jelly, 83
Salmon Salad, 81
Tuna Salad, 79
Sauces
Alfredo, 20
Florentine, 18
Lasagna, 19
Marinara, 21
Salmon, see fish and seafood
Shrimp, see fish and seafood
Snacks
Amelia's Deviled Eggs, 46
Buckwheat Thins, 178
Cheese Crackers with Flax Seeds, 177
Cottage Cheese and Dill Dip, 180
Crab Dip, 180
Dill Pickles, 181
Party Wings, 179
San Francisco French Garlic Spread, 176
Gilroy Garlic Growers Reply, 176
Soups
Cream of Celery Soup, 70
Cream of Chicken Soup, 71
Cream of Mushroom Soup, 72
French Onion Soup, 74
Pasta y Frigoli, Hearty Lentil Soup, 73
12 Minute Cream of Tomato Soup, 75
Spaghetti, see pastas
Spinach, see vegetables
Spreads, see snacks
Strawberries, see fruits
Tuna, see fish and seafood
Vegetables
Carrot Cake, 152
Cream of Celery Soup, 70
Cream of Chicken Soup, 71
Cream of Mushroom Soup, 72
Creamy Potatoes a& Broccoli Bake, 117
Dill Pickles, 181
Eggplant Parmesan, 138
French Onion Soup, 74
Pasta y Frigoli, Hearty Lentil Soup,
Spinach Salad, 60
Spinach Stuffed Lasagna Rolls, 91
Stuffed Peppers, 127
Vegetable Pasta Salad, 68
12 Minute Cream of Tomato Soup,
Waffles, 28
Yeast Breads, see breads